first edition

KEITH

Till I Roll Over Dead

Also by Stanley Booth:

The True Adventures of the Rolling Stones

KEITH

Till I Roll Over Dead

Stanley Booth

HEADLINE

First published in 1994 by
HEADLINE BOOK PUBLISHING

10 9 8 7 6 5 4 3 2 1

British Library Cataloguing in Publication Data

Booth, Stanley
Keith: Till I Roll Over Dead
I. Title
781.66092

ISBN 0–7472–0770–4

Phototypeset by Intype, London
Printed and bound in Great Britain by
Mackays of Chatham PLC, Chatham, Kent

HEADLINE BOOK PUBLISHING
A division of Hodder Headline PLC
338 Euston Road,
London NW1 3BH

Nobody can write the life of a man, but those who have eat and drunk and lived in social intercourse with him.

Sam Johnson,
Letter to Sir Joshua Reynolds, 31 March 1772

... one man in his time plays many parts ...

Shakespeare, *As You Like It*, II, vii

LIST OF ILLUSTRATIONS
Photographs: Bob Gruen

Black and white plate section 2

Keith on the 1981 US tour. He ripped a new tee-shirt every night.

1981, Madison Square Gardens. What Keith has is not grace, exactly, but whatever it is, it's very effective.

Keith and Bert Richards, New York City, September 1988. Estranged for two decades, Keith and his father now enjoy each other's company.

Keith, Tina Turner and Jack Daniels, backstage at the Ritz, New York, January 1983.

Keith grinning but not picking. February 1984, television interview with Lisa Robertson.

Keith, inspired by the Winos at New York's Beacon Theatre, February 1993, commences to trigger toe.

Keith and Patti gang up on Ron Wood – Stones party at Corso's, a Latin dance club on E86th St, New York, for the film *Let's Spend the Night Together*. February 1983.

'She's my little rock 'n' roll.' 'Patricia,' Keith says, 'is an amazing girl.'

Keith mangles a minor chord, Beacon Theatre, 1993.

Keith in February 1993, having yet another ecstatic moment.

CHAPTER 1

Actus non facit reum, nisi mens sit rea.

Anonymous

You don't know about me, and what is presently more to the point, you don't know about Keith Richards, without you have read a book called *The True Adventures of the Rolling Stones*. It is a mainly true book, with some stretchers, about these English boys, men, who called themselves that and played music and got to be hugely well known. That book has been cannibalized more times and has made more money for everybody save its author than he, that is, I, would care to count.

Keith's mother was born Doris Dupree thirty-three years before the birth of her only child, on December 18, 1943. That delivery took place at Livingstone Hospital in the London suburb of Dartford, Kent. Dartford lies fifteen miles to the east and slightly south of London on the way to Canterbury, an easy first stop for London pilgrims. Dartford has been inhabited since the Stone Age; Julius Caesar, following a battle nearby, decided to leave Kent and return to Gaul, and royalty has visited the town many times. Isabella, sister of Henry III, was married by proxy to the Emperor Frederick II of Germany in Dartford Church in 1235. Edward III held a tournament in Dartford in 1331 and later founded there the Dominican Priory. In 1415 Henry V passed through the

3

town on his return from Agincourt, and in 1422, his body rested in the Parish Church on its way to Westminster Abbey. During the Wars of the Roses (1452) Richard of York camped on the Brent and later surrendered to Henry VI at Dartford.

In Tudor times, Henry VIII built a manor house on the site of the Priory and there for some years lived the Lady Anne of Cleves after her divorce. Here, too, Elizabeth 'slept at her own house at Dartford,' in 1573.

Somehow these visits from royalty did not manage to impart to Dartford the same patina of fashion, elegance and ease that Cheltenham – Rolling Stone Brian Jones' hometown and another hangout for royals – is considered by many to have. Dartford is just a London suburb rather than a center of vacation landscape, and almost as regularly as there were royal visits there were rebellions. Dartford is closely associated with the Wat Tyler Rebellion of 1381. During this civil disturbance, Dartford featured as the rallying point for the rebels on two occasions, and a John Tyler of Dartford is supposed to have killed one of the government tax-collectors.

During the reign of Mary Tudor, Dartford was one of the many places where martyrs suffered for conscience' sake. The stake was set up at Dartford Brent, about three-quarters of a mile out of the town, along Watling Street. There, on July 17, 1555, Christopher Wade was burned as a heretic, and the memory of the Kent martyrs is perpetuated by a monument erected in the old burial ground on East Hill, which was the site of an ancient chapel of St. Edmund the Martyr and a place of pilgrimage in pre-Reformation times. In this reign too, two Dartford men – Robert Rudston and Thomas Fane – became involved in the Wyatt rebellion and were imprisoned in the Tower of London, where the inscriptions they carved may still be seen.

During the Civil War, the Lady Chapel in the Parish Church, which in 1642 had been converted into a powder magazine, was seized by the Kentish Royalists. At the time of the Restoration, Charles II passed through Dartford on his way to London. Stagecoaches started to run to Canterbury in 1670, and by 1815, seventy-two coaches were passing through the town every day. From a population of 2,406 in 1801, Dartford has grown to include over seventy thousand citizens. Its industries include cement manufacture, quarrying chalk, and papermaking; J. & E. Hall of Dartford is the world's foremost manufacturer of refrigeration plants for cargo ships, and Dartford is also an important center for the manufacture of drugs, zinc oxide, and fireworks. Almost the same percentage (one-tenth) of land in Dartford as in Cheltenham is devoted to parks and open spaces, but in Dartford most of the open spaces are playing fields, rather than flower gardens.

Few buildings of historical interest remain in Dartford, at least partly because of its having earned the name 'Doodle-bug Alley,' after the German unmanned rockets during World War Two. It was also called 'The Graveyard.'

Typically, Keith Richards, the ultimate rock 'n' roll survivor, who has been described as looking like an unresurrected Christ, remembers heroic occurrences from his early youth that didn't exactly happen.

'Even if I'm walking down a hotel corridor,' he told me, 'and somebody as I'm passing their room has the TV on, and it's playing one of those blitz movies, English war movies, and I hear that siren, there is nothing I can do about it. The hair goes up on the back of my head and I get goose bumps. It's a reaction, something that I picked up from what happened in the first eighteen months of my life, from other people that really knew what was going on. My old man was in the army, and my ma took me out shopping for an hour or two and a V1, you know, the doodlebug . . . we came back and the house was destroyed, it landed right on my crib. Adolf was on my tail. The bastard was after me. I

5

went up the road to my auntie's, 'cause we lived on the same street.'

The facts are less dramatic: The house was damaged but not destroyed, and it happened after Keith and his mother had been evacuated (an appropriate verb to describe the early activities of an artist never blind to the cloacal vision) to Mansfield, Nottinghamshire, where thirty-seven-year-old Bert Richards – Keith's father, his leg wounded in Normandy – was in hospital. ('Boris and Dirt,' Keith gave as his parents' names to a credulous fan mag.) The V1 raids lasted only two and a half months, and then Keith and his mother did go to stay with his aunt. 'We went up there,' Keith said, 'and lived with my aunt for the rest of the war, which was like for another nine months, this happened late '44. After the war was over – my first memory actually is looking up in the sky and sort of pointing up and my mom saying, "It's a Spitfire."

'After that I guess the memories start when I was three or four years old. I remember London, seeing these huge areas of rubble and grass growing and absolutely nothing. Dartford then was a very small town. You were on the edge of London but there was still plenty of space; you didn't actually feel part of London even though you were. When I was growing up, in those few years, if you went one way you went straight into the country and if you went towards London then you'd be in the suburbs in five or ten minutes. Dartford is a few miles from the Thames; all that's between Dartford and the river is just marshland. Which nobody has ever been able to do much with. We used to go down to the river when we were kids and play in these machine-gun bunkers and that was our playground, where weirdo hoboes would be living. Bums living in the marshes, and guys with shotguns. As I say, in Dartford you either go that way or you go in, and Dartford is one of those places where a lot of guys go out, they don't go in. No authority, none at all, just be the weirdest people living down there.

'The other reason that nobody would ever go near it was

that right on the river from Dartford, which I lived close to, this marshland, is the smallpox hospital . . . the plague joints. Built and left there, just in case an epidemic or something breaks out, lepers and . . . mud flats . . . The Thames – the river's how you find out how to get to London from the air, it's easy to spot. It's like, "This way." But it's not very habitable land, so it's like five gunpowder factories, armament factories; they make fireworks in peacetime, if it's wartime, they're just makin' powder. There's power stations and cement works on the horizon and nothing else except geese, little streams, marshes, marshland.'

In 1954, with his family, the eleven-year-old Mick Jagger – who would become Keith Richards' songwriting collaborator and fellow band member in the Rolling Stones – moved to Wilmington, just outside Dartford in Southeast London. The year before, Keith Richards, six months Mick's junior, had come with his mother and father to live in a Dartford council estate that Keith would later characterize as 'soul-destroying.'

'When I met Mick,' Keith said, 'I was living on the other side of town to where we eventually ended up. I first met Mick in 1949 or 1950, if not a little earlier. We went to our first school together at five, and he used to live around the corner from me, so we used to run into each other on our tricycles, and hang around here and there.

'Rationing lasted until 1954, so World War Two went on for people of my generation for another nine years after it finished everywhere else. That's when finally the candy came off rationing. When you're a kid growing up, that's the big thing. You can get more than one little bag a week, if you've got the bread, suddenly you can buy as much as you want. I remember when I first went to school, for months and months you got a bottle of concentrated orange juice – that

7

was the only time you saw it – against the scurvy. Used to come in medicine bottles in England; you'd get them from the school medical services.'

Untypically, Keith, who would become famous as the soul of rebellion, of rock 'n' roll, spent his early adolescent years as a ball boy (Bert played tennis) and a choir boy. 'Every weekend that the weather was nice – I had no choice, you know,' Keith explains. 'It was just a little two-court tennis court in Sidcup, where I ended up going to art school. About ten miles from home, I could ride a bike. Nice bunch of people, cricket club across the way. That's what I did on the weekends. We'd be there and if they had some competition and they needed ball boys, I would play ball boy. From seven, eight until . . . thirteen, fourteen, fifteen.'

As a choir boy, Keith said, 'I used to wear the cassock and everything, the whole bit. I can even remember the choirmaster's name, Jake Clair. But at that age, twelve or thirteen . . . you're gonna sing, it's just a trip out; but you find out later on that you actually sang for the Queen in the Royal Festival Hall or Westminster Abbey. All my gigs since have gone right downhill. I forgot about it for thirty years, but me and two other guys did soprano, just a trio; the three of us did a whole trip down the aisle at Westminster Abbey, I guess it was about 1956 or 1957. We were the three worst kids, the worst hoods in the school in our own ways. But we had these three angelic voices. And Jake Clair had been working on us for a couple of years by then; you'd get taken on the bus with the choir, to compete with this school and that school and what I didn't realize until very recently was how good that guy must have been to get this little suburban choir into places like that. To us it was a way of getting out of chemistry and physics classes; if you were in the choir you could get out of doing some of the more boring subjects.

'I had been in that choir two or three years, and once the voice broke there was no choir. So suddenly you're thrown back into the full curriculum and at first I was sort of resentful, being thrown out of the choir. Jake Clair had to be hard. I'm sure it broke his heart in many ways because the sopranos only last so long when they're boys... If you've got a soprano and he's eighteen years old, baby, he's got a problem. At the same time, it was the first time, like, "We'll call you." And so, immediately, the next year I fucked up royally. I was resentful, I had to do all this shit that I'd managed to get out of. So then they sent me to art school.

'In art school there's a very free atmosphere, you could walk into the john to take a pee and there would be three guys sitting around playing the guitar. They'd skip life class and they're doing like Woody Guthrie and Jack Elliott stuff. I didn't learn much about art in art school, but I did learn a lot about guitar playing. 'Cause then ... in the john you get the underground. You get into "Talkin' New York Blues," "Mule Skinner Blues," and "Cocaine" – the song, not the stuff at the time. I was getting very interested in the blues, doing the Big Bill Broonzy, Muddy Waters stuff through listening to these cats play, and listening to like Jessie Fuller, twelve-string stuff, "Stagolee." '

The strongest influence from Keith's family was his grandfather. 'Gus – Augustus Theodore Dupree – was me mother's father. My granddad's name was DuPree because they were French, but they were protestant French and they got blown out and so they moved to the channel islands, the islands between England and France and they came from there to England. He was a musician, a guy who could do anything, just about. If he can't do it, give him somebody to talk to and he'll talk him into doing it. He had seven daughters, and obviously he was living with the wife, so he's in a house full of eight women. It's enough to drive any guy barmy, that ... And the only way around that is a sense of humor, which he had an abundance of.

'My aunts and uncles told me about the things he got up to when they started getting to the dating age. With seven daughters there were like four boyfriends around the front steps at once, and Gus would put a fucking used rubber on a piece of string and dangle it from an upstairs window so all the boys would see it – anything to fox 'em. He was one of the great dirty old men – I'm still trying to figure him out. See, when you know your family . . . it's usually after they're dead and gone that you start to really appreciate them and suss out all the ramifications that they were trying to lay on you. At the time, "There's Granddad and he's my granddad and I'm gonna do what he says." Then you start to understand, they're fuckin' gurus. Just your granddad, or dad, or your auntie, they can teach this shit and they'll do it in a way . . . they know what they're doing. You don't realize what it is they've done. I still sit here realizing things that my grandfather did. Just startin' to cotton on to the angle that he laid on me . . .

'He was a saxophone player, also a master baker, and in the First World War he got gassed, chlorine shit, and after that he couldn't work in a bakery or play the sax anymore. The lungs were gone. So he took up the fiddle and guitar and piano, he used to have bands in the thirties. Later on, in the fifties, he played American G.I. bases in England, with a sort of western swing band, real hokey shit really, "Turkey in the Straw," good enough for the fifties.

'When I'd go to visit him, first off he'd feed me, then I'd just look at this guitar. I always thought it lived on top of the piano. In actual fact it was always in its case and when he knew I was coming over, he would for some reason take it out, polish it up, display it. Never pushed it on me. He never said, "You should do this," he would just leave it there as a sort of icon, just resting on the wall, on top of the piano . . . and I would always look at it – and, like, the guy was a smart guy. He waited for years and years for me to say, "What's that? can I . . .?" Never tried to force it on me at all. He started that shit when I was about six, seven. I must have been twelve, thirteen, it must have been after my choir years. Before that I wasn't into instruments, I was just into singing. I guess he caught me at the point where I had to transfer any interest into playing instrumental music.

'It happened in a very smooth way, because I had been going to art school for a couple of years and my grandfather had eventually turned me on to the guitar and given me a few pointers, and said, "Play this for me," as if I was doing him a favor. I was really bad, I had only just started playing, but he would sit back and say, "Play 'Malagueña.' If you can play that you can play anything." It's a great exercise, and no matter how badly I played it, he would lie back, sit back in his chair and keep his eyes closed and nod. I mean, it must have been *appalling*. And every time, he would pretend he liked the way I played it, and so, wow, I'm turnin' my granddad on – which is an amazing way of teaching things.

'I used to hang around with him, he would take me around London, we'd be in Charing Cross Road in the back of Ivor Marantz's guitar store where they're repairing instruments. I used to sit for hours and hours in the back rooms in these guitar shops, in the middle of London, with the glue boiling and bubbling away and they're repatching guitars, down in some little basement somewhere – it's like Santa's workshop. These guitars are hanging up and varnish is going on, wonderful smells in the air. To watch for two or three hours while these guys take this mashed-up old violin apart and make it come alive again in front of your eyes. Steam's going down, they're pressing wood, and patching, it's amazing, like some alchemist's laboratory for me at the time.

'And around 1956, I heard "Heartbreak Hotel," and the world suddenly went Technicolor. Candy came off rationing, rock 'n' roll arrived, and suddenly there's color. During this time, I saw Mick only by accident. I once saw him outside the Dartford Library selling ice creams – he had a summer job there with a little trolley, refrigerator.' ('It may come to

11

that again,' I said.) 'Yeah, I hope he remembers the moves. Anyway, in a town like Dartford, if anybody's working in London or anyplace in between, at Dartford Station you're bound to meet. So one day I ran into Mick there and he had two albums with him: *Rocking at the Hops*, by Chuck Berry, and *The Best of Muddy Waters* – and I had only heard about Muddy up to that point, I'd never actually heard him. I didn't get to that day, obviously, we're on the goddamn train. But I tell Mick I know all Chuck Berry's licks, and he says, "What you play, guitar?" I said yeah. He had a little youth-club band that he was working with at the time, doing like Buddy Holly and Eddie Cochran stuff, but Mick was very heavily into blues. He had bothered to figure out how to get it together.

'Me, I wasn't at that stage, I was never that organized, still ain't. Scotty Moore, with Elvis, was my man at the time. I knew Big Bill Broonzy, Josh White, Leadbelly. My mother brought me up more on people like Ella Fitzgerald, Sarah Vaughan, Billy Eckstine, Basie, Ellington, a lot of Nat [King] Cole. It was a very musical family, they just loved music. You see, to me, the art of music is listening to it, not playing it. The real art of it is hearing it. And then if you have a facility and the opportunity that way, then maybe you get around to playing it, but the number of people who make music compared with the number of people who listen to it is minimal. So what I guess you're trying to do is tickle those ears out there in one way or another, see if I can get inside you one way or another.'

CHAPTER 2

This new style had a magical and stimulating effect upon audiences everywhere, and no less upon the musicians themselves. When Panassie visited New York in 1938 a group of musicians, including the late Tommy Ladnier and Mezz Mezzrow, were assembled in a recording studio for a session. At that time 'Hold Tight' was the hit song of the moment. One of the musicians started to play the second phrase from this tune, 'I Want Some Sea Food Mama.' The seven notes sounded wonderful, constituting a perfect riff. The musicians kept repeating it; Mezzrow, too, joined in, and Tommy Ladnier added himself to the ensemble. Panassie started to sing along with them, and the whole bunch, possessed by this riff delirium, completely forgot about the matter of making records.

Robert Goffin, *Jazz*

'Mick and I met on the train around '60 or '61, somewhere around there,' Richards remembered. 'We talked, we kicked around a band for a summer or so with Dick Taylor who was later in the Pretty Things and Phil May. Dick Taylor went to the same school as Mick; Phil May was at art school with me. David Bowie went to the same school a year or so after I left.

'About '61 or '62, Alexis Korner gets going with a band called Blues, Incorporated, which included Cyril Davies, from Wembley, a great panelbeater and great harp player, beloved by Sonny Terry and Sonny Boy Williamson, who both taught him. He wouldn't take shit from nobody. Big motherfucker too, and here I am some little skinny seventeen- or eighteen-year-old – "Fuck off, get away, kid, get away." He had no mercy for anybody, another hard teacher. When he left Alexis's band he put together the Cyril Davies All-Stars, with Nicky Hopkins. An all-time maestro, but an absolute terror.

'Very soon after Mick and I re-met, within a few months there's an ad in the music papers, "England's First Rhythm & Blues Club Opening Up" – but it's in West London. When you're still in school and not making bread it's hard to get there. Mick comes from a better part of town than I do, a fairly swanky area, and he's got a house that's all by itself with a garage. The whole bit, because Mick's dad, Joe, was a very well respected physical education instructor, used to go to America to referee matches, stuff like that. Mick had a much broader education than I did. If I got out of Dartford it was just to get on my bike and go to Sidcup, or to go down to my granddad's for a few days in London, and that would be about it. I was workin' class, and to me, Mick, and the friends and the chicks that he knew, it was like, "Wow, really movin' up in society." From this fucking council house to this whole part of town; even though it's my town, I had been living there eighteen years, it's a part I never go to, I didn't know anyone there.

'So Alexis's club comes together, the Ealing Club, and we said, "We've got to go see this," and Mick actually managed to borrow his dad's car. Big deal, I'm going into town, it's my first trip into town just to have some fun, and of course it's a revelation because it was a small joint, the band is cooking, Jack Bruce is on bass, Brian was there, he played some Elmore James shit which was sheerly electrifying, to see somebody play slide steel guitar in England at that time was absolutely amazing. And Charlie Watts is on drums and this suddenly opens up a whole new world, 'cause everybody in this place is there because they're interested in the same kind of music. I was hooked from that minute on, not just – From the music, I was already hooked, but it was like a musician's club, it was like I was in the union without a card. Stu was there that night too. Alexis Korner put a place together where everybody that was interested would all come together, and so half of the influence of popular music all over the world comes from that little joint. He made a little cauldron for everybody to boil up in and get their licks down, and if he thought you were interesting, he'd take you home and feed you. A real gent. Alexis was no great player, nor singer, but he did have the necessary credentials within the London music circles to be able to start something. I think he knew exactly what he was doing. He was another great teacher.

'Well, we heard Brian play, then we started to talk the next week and then Alexis invited Mick and me to come up and play, which we did. Also, to finance this venture, Alexis swung real quick on the PR job and it became like the hip place. Even though it was a total dump under a subway station, it became the place where they – and the sixties are so far away – but it sort of became the debutante slumming joint. All these chicks! Lady So-and-so – you get a quick education on what a lady is. They would have these deb balls and parties and it turned into a society band and Mick would sing for them, because Alexis immediately realized that Mick . . . raw as it was, it could easily magnetize. What he's trying to do is put this music across. Afterwards, what we all turned out to do, our job – I left art school, decided to actually live with the other guys and try to be a rhythm & blues band, if you will, rather than spend three years in art school and look for a job as tea boy in some advertising agency. They start you from the ground up in those joints.

'This cat Brian Keogh who taught me, he had that cynical eye: "You think you're an artist – you're a fucking advertiser, that's what you are, boy." Little bloke in a bow tie, snotty little turd, but he was good at what he did. He knew what he was supposed to produce. What he was trying to do was produce cats who could fill in the agencies, do the work, make the ads happen. He saw this as the new art form, the new canvas. At the time I thought, "What a snotty man in his bow tie and fucking mustard vest, a right hooray," but the guy knew – "Just design another record cover, Richards. Put it where your heart is . . . Start with doing the gin adverts." I can still go into a darkroom and do the shit, matter of exposures and length of times of development. You learn certain things and you apply them to other parts of your life as you go along. My outlook was . . . I'd been more and more and more putting everything I had ... into the guitar.'

◙

'So in fact, the very first night that Mick and I went to this joint, we walked in, there were Charlie, Stu, and Brian. At that time you have to remember, in '61, '62, Elvis is in the army, Buddy and Eddie are dead, Chuck's in jail, Jerry Lee is disgraced, and Little Richard has thrown his rings in the water. But to us, being English, this thing made our world come into sort of Cinemascope, full Technicolor, where before it was just drab, scraping – and we are not about to let this motherfucker go. Also, in place of the giants who are not around anymore, Tin Pan Alley had moved back in and you were getting Bobby Vee, Fabian, Frankie Avalon – I don't want to knock these cats, but – the records they were making, it was like, bring the violin and the chimes back in, we're gonna move in and make some really bad rock 'n' roll.

'The situation in England was that if you wanted to be a rock 'n' roll band, then you came under the influence of the big promoters, the strong-arm boys, which meant that you played three or four ballrooms a night in a certain area, forty-five minutes onstage, you get off, jump in the car and are driven to another one, and then back to the other one for the second show later on. You wear shitty little suits that they advance you money on and then charge you for later, and wear and tear, and if you don't make the gig they break your fucking leg. Also, you play the Top Twenty, which means playing "Rubber Ball Bouncing Back to You" instead of "That'll Be the Day." The only possible way out of that is to go with the other zone, which happens in England to be the students and the people who are not any way gonna go to ballrooms. It's a class thing. Kids that go to university, college, art school, are not going to go to a ballroom where all these chicks with beehives and tight miniskirts, and guys looking for a fight, thugs, are gonna hang out. It never pays off that way, 'cause there are thugs everywhere and chicks are like that no matter what they wear. Nevertheless, ballrooms weren't appealing to these people, they felt intellectually superior.

'Basically what happened was that when rock 'n' roll took that dive for a year or two around 1960, they took up Dixieland, what the English called traditional jazz. There were some good players in England and these guys set up this whole club network throughout the country – Acker Bilk, Kenny Ball, were selling big even in the United States, scoring with records like "Midnight in Moscow" and "Petites Fleurs." They'd come out of this second mainstream of possible ways to play music in England. It was the only possible one apart from – If you wanted to be a guitar player and play rock 'n' roll, you either played these ballrooms, got your leg broke if you missed the gig, or you went somewhere else, found other alternatives. What happened, once this rhythm & blues thing started, with Alexis and then ourselves on the scene, a year later we're in competition with these jazz cats.

'And once again Alexis did the main job by going straight to the Marquee, the biggest jazz club in England, on Thursday nights, and that's when they get the joint filled up, suddenly the thing's taking off. They'd have big names in on the weekends, but on Friday and Saturday they were not getting as many people as for this little rhythm & blues session on a Thursday. That's when the joint starts rocking. Things start to snowball, other joints in town saying, "Well, if they're doing that there, maybe we should have a rhythm & blues night" – so suddenly there are some gigs around. Also you're in direct conflict with these other musicians and these other types of promoters in the jazz scene, well-entrenched, top hands, top players, and suddenly we're taking their living away from them. Suddenly you're looking at something big, and Alexis has done all of this.

'We're still toying, kicking around the idea of putting a band together. We rehearsed for, must have been nine months before we got a regular gig. We've talked to Brian a few times over the first weekends, and Stu – Stu and Brian knew each other already – and then we had a talk with the drummer, Charlie Watts, who to us is *the* guy. He would haul his drums around the subways of London for fun. He had already a very well established career, that couldn't go anywhere but up, in advertising – J. Walter Thompson or one of the other big agencies, he was well in there . . . but Charlie hates advertising, he hates anything phony. He has an incredible line, his stuff is quite amazing – it's all a matter of touch, with Charlie. Whether it's a pencil or a drumstick, it's all a matter of touch and tension, not notes. But when we met him, he already had some good-paying music gigs, he's Alexis's drummer, why the fuck does he want to play with some snotty little kids? Charlie's already hip, he's got suits and ties, he's already like a Harlem hipster and so for us he's unattainable, he's a lovely guy, but he's already got a gig. But he also knows Stu, and somehow he's very interested in us even though there is no way he can actually play with a band that hasn't got a gig.

'Also hanging out around there around this time is another load of cats, Blues by Five. Brian Knight, who is a lovely bloke, like Gene Vincent with red hair, he loved the blues, he's so London – with Geoff Bradford, finger picker on the electric guitar, astounding. Brian knows these cats and Stu knows them and they are talking about putting a band together and then Mick and I get up to play at Alexis' club, and they go Ohh . . . Nobody's too sure about me, I'm too rock 'n' roll, I'm not pure enough. Also, I'm being very flash with it. At that time in London you only had to play one Chuck Berry number for the whole club to divide into sides as to whether Chuck Berry was either rock 'n' roll or rhythm & blues. Stupid question, but bless their hearts, people were into it.

20

'Nobody could imagine the scene ever getting much bigger. You figure maybe you can live, you can exist on three or four club gigs a week in London. You don't see ever gettin' out because the rest of the country's so unhip, this is strictly Capitol City shit. Not for the masses, not when you hear what they're listening to. "I'm a Pink Toothbrush." It's already back to "How Much is that Doggy in the Window?", that sort of thing. Not totally because there were some very hot and great rock 'n' roll bands around. You had Nero and the Gladiators, incredible players. Johnny Kidd and the Pirates were great players. What Cyril Davies did was hire Screamin' Lord Sutch's band in total. They were just glad they didn't have to watch this guy burn a coffin every god-damn gig. And Ricky Fenson and Carlo Little, they were the ones who gave us the power shot. I think Carlo's a butcher now, and Ricky runs a garage or something. Ricky Fenson, bleached hair. His hair was black but was peroxide blond. Him and another guy called Bernie, they used to call Straw-berry, the guitar player. I wish I could remember his last name. He would sit on a stage with his gloves on his head, on this peroxide thing, 'cause he had the same hairdo as Ricky Fenson. Bernie. What a guitar player. I thought, "Well, I might as well go home, this is ridiculous, this cat's so good." Cyril Davies put that band together – listen to a record called "Country Line Special" by Cyril Davies's All-Stars, with Nicky Hopkins, Bernie, Ricky Fenson and Carlo Little.

'So, Mick and I had been working with Dick Taylor, back-room stuff, and it's gettin' better. Then we go down to hear Alexis, meet Brian and Stu, and I have the feeling I am grudgingly invited to this rehearsal, for a possible alternative – other band to Alexis and Cyril's setup.

'The first rehearsal for the Stones or what turned out to be the Stones was at a place called the Bricklayer's Arms, just off Wardour Street in London. It was a pretty exotic area for me at the time. I mean, these chicks walking by in full

21

makeup with just a bra on, carryin' a suitcase. It took me a while to figure it out, but they're strippers going from one club to another. They just crisscross, do like half an hour here and another half hour down the street, so they don't bother to dress, just as long as they don't get arrested for indecent exposure, they're just rushing out in their dressing gowns with the suitcase and a wig and the makeup. Maybe it looks great inside of the club but outside not quite so good, these weird masked people coming at you.

'I got my guitar in a little plastic case, and I go upstairs and say – some old barmaid was there, typical English platinum blonde with a cigarette, her lipstick smeared – "We're supposed to have a room to rehearse in here." "Upstairs, second floor." I tramp up there and I hear this piano playing, so I follow that. I walk in and there's Stu sitting there and the piano is against the window and he's playing beautifully as Stu always did when he thought nobody was listening. That's the area where he really breaks out. To hear Stu play under observation is only half of what he is capable of. He was never a showman. It locks him up, to have people watch him, he is his own audience.

'So he's playin' this Pinetop and St. Louis Jimmy shit and I'm following this piano walkin' and there is Stu in little leather shorts. He's playin' this shit but obviously he's not particularly thinkin' about it – he's staring intently out of the window and I don't know ... I'm tryin' to figure out what the fuck it is. I didn't want to disturb him 'cause he's playing this great shit and I don't know what the hell I'm supposed to be doing there because I already know that I'm the Chuck Berry player and he don't think shit of me. I know this. I mean I've already got the vibes from other guys that I'm some rock 'n' roller and I'm not a bluesman. I should be working the ballrooms. It's touch and go ... and I realize that he is staring at his bicycle which is propped up against the wall across the street so that nobody steals it. He could do that. He could play security and incredible boogie-woogie at the same time. I still haven't said anything; I just slipped into the room and he doesn't know I'm there, I got the guitar under the arm, still watching him, I don't want to break this music, and I hear him go, "Cor, look a' that." I crane my neck a bit around behind him and here's one of the strippers walking down the road, and he hadn't dropped a beat.

'I'd just seen him a couple of times with Korner, he would come up and do a couple of numbers, but to me this guy is The Boss. I'm just a kid like crawling in, and I don't even have the balls to cough, or go back out and knock. So I'm just standin' there for five or ten minutes, and every now and again he would go, "Oh, look at that." Immediately I'm in love with this guy and – I'm still not really sure whether to interrupt him, because I've already found out more about him, in just a few minutes . . . I mean now I've really fucked up because I've got to get out of here and now I'm like spying. It's like catching some guy jerking off. Finally he stopped and turned and said, "Oh, you're the Chuck Berry artist." I knew I was under heavy penalties.

'Mick [was] working with Alexis on selected high-society dates, deb weddings,' Keith said. 'Then Alexis had to do the BBC live broadcast, and we filled in for him at the Marquee Club, the first Stones gig. For some reason Alexis used Ginger Baker on drums for the broadcast and Charlie played with us. Charlie had obviously gotten his first inclination that everything is not totally stable, and Mick doesn't know whether to hang with Alexis or whether to try out for this new band, like with his new old friend, so there's a lot of undercurrent. Brian is playing everything against the middle. He's workin' in Whitely's, rippin' off records, getting accused of stealing cash from the till – which he was doing – and living with this chick and a baby in the utmost squalor. His second baby; his first one is back somewhere with its mother in the Cheltenham hills, the Cotswolds. Brian is a little older than me, not that much [Brian Jones was born February 29, 1942], but he's already payin' rent, and he's got two kids.

I'm just out of art school with nothing in particular to do. I don't know what the hell I'm gonna do. I know what I want to do, but I don't know whether it would be possible to put it together.'

CHAPTER 3

Keith is the only one who is not naturally middle class. Keith is a man of belief. This is meant merely by way of contrast. Keith is a man of belief and Mick is a man of fear. Mick works on fear, that driving thing, 'What if I fuck up?' It's a lot easier to be like Keith than it is to be like Mick.

Alexis Korner,
in Barbara Charone's *Keith Richards*

'At the start,' the wonderfully opinionated Stu told me, 'nobody in England played this kind of music. But nobody. Brian, Mick, and Keith, they were the only ones. When I first saw Mick with Alexis Korner, winter '61, they were trying to play a sort of Muddy Waters thing, but it didn't really come off. They had Jackie Bruce on bass, who was very modern-inclined – and every number they played that Dick Heckstall-Smith'd stand up and play some terrible saxophone. It was a terrible mixture. The only one in that band who really knew the style was that guy Cyril Davies, who was a very, very good harmonica player. Korner is the worst guitar player in the world and his singing is pathetic. Korner's one of these guys who irritate me a lot because he likes everything. When Korner decided he wanted an r&b band, he picked up Jackie Bruce, who'd been playing in a trad band, who's a solid bass player. But don't forget that none of the Jimmy Reed records – there might have been four Muddy Waters titles available, there might have been four Little Walter titles available, and that was it. In 1961 Mick had reels of Jimmy Reed tapes, Elmore James's "The Sun is Shining," a lot of unissued Muddy Waters and Little Walter stuff, and Slim Harpo. Unless you were a real enthusiast, like Cyril or Alexis or Mick – none of these other guys had ever heard the music.

'Cyril and Alexis had this duo thing going on accoustic guitar and harmonica – rather after Brownie [McGhee] and Sonny [Terry] fashion but they knew a lot of other things besides, certainly since 1955–56, probably before that. They'd been playin' in pubs, and then they got it into their heads that they wanted to form an r&b band. But their idea of an r&b band was the sort of Joe Turner thing where you get the "Roll 'em, Pete" vocals, you get an earthy tenor sax, a blues piano and a heavy rhythm. But the rhythm was a jazz thing, with just an offbeat. They had Bruce and for a while they had Charlie [Watts], but Charlie had never heard the music either, didn't have the foggiest idea. It was a sort of jazz rhythm section.

'Mick went to Alexis – Mick and Keith for a kickoff were Chuck Berry fans – so when they went along and sat in with Alexis, Mick always wanted to do "Sweet Little Sixteen," because Keith knew it off pat. And of course all these guys who were playing with Alexis thought it was rock 'n' roll. Cyril thought it was too commercial, it wasn't really pure enough – Mick would do Jimmy Reed things and they'd back him all right, and then Mick would want to bring Keith up and go into the Berry stuff, but Charlie and them were still trying to play *ching-ching-ching* to the Berry stuff 'cause they'd never heard his beat before, and it all got to be a bit weird.

'I'll never forget the first time I saw Mick, though. 'Cause I could only see his head above a crowd of people – and I thought, "Fuck me, there's a guy who's gonna go a long way." 'Cause he looked so good even then, he didn't just stand there and sing, he moved. Mick can't sing to save his fuckin' life, and he's a fantastic performer.'

In the May 19, 1962, issue of *Disc*, a small news item appeared: 'Singer joins Korner's Blues, Inc.' The singer was Mick Jagger.

'Then,' Stu said, 'as Mick and Brian saw more of each other through Korner – y'see, Mick didn't really like what Korner was doin' because of the jazz end of it, influence in it, because Mick doesn't really like jazz, and Mick and this other guitar player didn't get on at all. So then, when Mick started comin' to our little things – 'cause Brian was keen and we used to blow with different people three times a week, at a pub in Lyle Street was one place, another place was just across the street from where Trident Studio is now – Brian brought Mick along quite often, and then Mick said, "I'm not doin' it unless Keith's doin' it"

'So then there was Mick and Keith and Brian and me. And then the big search for a bass and drummer. We were still only rehearsin', we didn't have a name or anything. As soon as Keith started showin' up regularly, this Dick Taylor guy came with him. I couldn't figure all this out, they used to walk in with amplifiers and speakers, and I'd never even seen these things before, and I could never understand why Dick's guitar only had four strings. But I didn't go into that, I thought it was none of my business. We started tryin' out all these different bloody drummers all the time, and it was really heartbreaking, used to get a lot of people interested in playin', but none of them had any idea.'

Alexis Korner, like the father of Humbert Humbert 'a salad of racial genes' – the Paris-born son of a Turkish-Greek mother and an Austrian father; 'probably Jewish, it never seemed important' – was raised in France, Switzerland, North Africa, and finally, England, where he became one of the first Europeans to play American-style blues. 'In 1940,' Korner said [that is, when he was about ten years old], 'I came across a record by Jimmy Yancey. I can't say how important that record is. From then on all I wanted to do was play the blues. When Jimmy Blanton died, I wore a

29

black armband. Three of us did all day at school.'

Korner left the family shipping firm [he'd been thrown out of St. Paul's for nonconformity and sent to Finsden Manor School, for disturbed boys with high IQs, and there he'd made a guitar out of plywood and a table leg], became an A&R man at Melodisc Records, then a publicist at Decca and a studio manager at the BBC. In 1949, Korner replaced Lonnie Donegan in the first band led by Chris Barber, another English fanatic. Donegan was going into the army as Korner was coming out. Barber's band was a traditional jazz organization – traditional meaning Dixieland twenties' and thirties' style – but it included a blues quartet that played on gigs for about half an hour as a separate unit. At the time, the music that would be called blues, rhythm & blues, and soul, was referred to as race music. 'We had the first race quartet in England,' Korner said, 'playing Big Maceo and Tampa Red numbers within a year of their being released. We cut no records. The personnel was Chris Barber on bass, Roy Sturges on piano, Brian somebody was the drummer, I played guitar, we all sort of sang. Then Ken Colyer, who'd been trotting in and out of New Orleans as a merchant seaman came back to England and formed a jazz band with Chris Barber: Ken; Chris; Lonnie Donegan, when he got out of the army, on washboard; I played guitar, mandolin, and banjo. We were sort of the Colyer-Barber Jazz Band Skiffle Group.

'So, as had happened before – I'd left the Chris Barber band just before it became really successful – I managed to leave this skiffle group just before Lonnie Donegan made "Rock Island Line." When the money is just starting, I leave. It's not intentional, it's just the way it's happened, always. At that time I was just sitting at home playing guitar. My wife forced me to learn proper tuning while I was with the group. I was very set on country blues at the time, Broonzy mania – Bill used to live with us when he was over, in our spare room. That's where my children had an advantage, because my daughter used to be sung to sleep by Bill Broonzy, from about the age of six. He'd go into his room and rehearse the songs before he'd sing them to her. He'd run over the songs for fifteen or twenty minutes and then he'd go in and take his guitar and sit down by the side of her bed and play three or four songs and then walk out. He was one of the most amazing human beings I've ever met.

'I was working for the BBC at the time I went up to the Roundhouse in Wardour Square, a pub in which the London Skiffle Club was on the first floor. Cyril Davies played with the skiffle group there, and we got closer and closer together – within a matter of minutes. And after a time, Cyril, who was a very, very strong person indeed, managed to talk all the others into closing down the London Skiffle Club and us reopening it as the London Blues and Barrelhouse Club. This was at the height of the skiffle movement, and the club, which had been crowded solid every night it was open, suddenly had about fifteen people in it. There were Squyril and I playing the blues and nobody, but nobody, wanted to know. We played on for years, I can't remember how many, every Thursday night, and John Baldry used to come up, he was about fifteen at the time, sixteen, and he used to come in and sing. He always had a good voice. Sonny [Terry] and Brownie [McGhee] on their first tour were made honorary presidents of the club, and they always played the club for nothing. We used to get a bottle of scotch in for each of them, and every Thursday night when they were over, it was a blowing night. Then we all used to go back to the house that I had at the time and have an all-night party.

'We used to buy about forty pounds' weight of bacon hocks and boil them all up and get in barrels and barrels of cheap wine and beer and about fifty or sixty people would show up on the Thursday nights – we'd done quite well by then – it was the only live club performance Muddy made in London on his first tour in '58, when he was still a great singer, and that was the best Otis Spann I ever heard in my

31

life, at that period. Muddy came over playing electric guitar and he got practically booed off the stage at St. Pancras Town Hall because he was playing electric. That was the stage Cyril and I were at, because we wanted to play electric and none of the clubs outside our own would let us into the place with an amplifier. The only place you could play blues in those days was in trad jazz clubs, and they would not accept electric guitars as instruments. You could use a P.A. system if you absolutely had to, but you were certainly not allowed to use an amplified guitar. We got thrown out of several clubs for using electric guitar.

'Charlie [Watts] and I first met when he was playing drums at the Troubadour in 1960–61. There was a small jazz group down at the Troubadour, and Charlie used to play drums. I used to float down; Eric Lindstrum was singing down there and Bernie Newman was playing trombone with various odd people. It was a sort of a Thelonious Monk-style group, and I played guitar, because I liked playing all that stuff. They were playing Monk numbers and [Charlie] Parker numbers, and doing things to old blues numbers. I liked Charlie's drumming, he was a nice brush drummer.' [Charlie told me about the first night Alexis came in with his guitar and a tiny little amplifier which Alexis hung on the wall behind Charlie's drums – and Charlie, offended at this taste-lessness, this uncalled-for amplification, took the amp off the wall.]

'Eventually I asked Charlie, "If I form a blues band, would you like to come in as drummer?" and Charlie said yes, so that's how, about February '62, Charlie and I got together. He was working in an advertising agency at the time. The band that opened the club at Ealing was in fact Charlie, Andy Hooganboom on bass – Andy taught at one of the art schools – Dick Heckstall-Smith on tenor, Cyril, Keith Scott on piano, and me on guitar.

'And then the rhythm section changed 'round because Andy wasn't good enough and Jack Bruce came in instead of Andy. Jack was playing with the Scottsville Jazzmen at the time, and they'd only got about one gig a week, so he made both. And then he joined us full time. He was into Ealing by the second or third week, I should think. Mick was into the club almost from the beginning, sort of standing around waiting to sing his three songs every night – "Sweet Honey Bee," Muddy's thing, some Vee-Jay song, used to do the odd Bo Diddley song when Cyril wasn't listening. Cyril didn't like that stuff at all. In fact, he was rather cross with me over introducing what he maintained were rock 'n' roll elements into the band.

'Brian was just part of the dozen or so people – Brian, Mick, Keith, Cyril, Jack, Ginger, Long John, Dick Heckstall, Graham Bond – who were around together and played together and talked the music over. At first you got the impression that Keith was just trailing around with Mick. The first fifteen minutes he was trailing around but it didn't take any longer to realize Keith wasn't trailing around at all. He just happened to be quieter. Keith never appeared without Mick. The first day they came to see me it was Mick and Keith. And it was *always* Mick and Keith. Always. Keith never thought of it as Mick's band. We opened the Marquee in May '62. By then Manfred Mann and Eric Burdon were coming down to sit in, so you could always get people in to get a good blow going. Used to get some very good things going when everyone did it just because they wanted to do it. There's always a difference which comes in when there's bread involved.

'It'd get wound up sometimes and really move rather well. Eric [Clapton] at that time couldn't play the guitar at all. He bought a guitar after the band started at the Marquee – used to come up and ask us what guitar strings to buy – and he used to show up on the Tuesday nights at the Ealing Club in a pair of white plimsolls and look at them all night, and sing "Roll Over, Beethoven," which was the only song he knew, and then retire. Used to call him Plimsolls. He'd stand up there lookin' down at his shoes and singin' "Roll Over, Beethoven."'

'There were jokes about Clapton,' Stu said, ''cause his parents had a bit of money and they bought him this new Kay guitar, so every time Keith or Brian's guitar went up the wall they'd start talking nicely to this Clapton and borrow his new guitar for the night.'

'At the Ealing Club,' Alexis said, 'we used to stretch a tarpaulin – 'cause the stage part of the club used to run under the pavement, and there was one of those glass skylights over the top to let light in, and you know how condensation forms under those. If we didn't stretch a tarpaulin over the skylight the stage was flooded and all the amps shorted out. So what we had to do was stretch that tarpaulin over, and after a packed Saturday night with a lot of people in, we used to take the tarpaulin out and empty it in the street and bring it in and hang it up again until Tuesday when the Stones did it. The other clubs in the majority of cases had fairly low ceilings, pretty sweaty working conditions, difficult acoustics, always very bad, if any, dressing rooms – mostly 'cause people didn't consider you needed a dressing room.

'We played a lot of makeshift sports clubs, sort of a shingle-built cricket pavilion which you might play in for the cricket-club dance and the walls would start to shake the moment you'd put on more than ten watts of anything. Most of the time you'd have to plug into an electric light socket. After we got a few shocks we learned to stay well back. That is to say, you could grab a mike as long as you weren't holding a guitar at the same time. The working conditions were in keeping with the music we were playing, which was hot, sweaty, uncomfortable music. The Marquee had the best working conditions of any London club as far as dressing rooms, stage, were concerned.

'They were all pretty grotty. Eel Pie was grotty, the floor gave way after a while so they had to close it and open it again with new floors. Richmond Station Hotel was a pub, a pub room; changing rooms – there weren't any. It was the gents' lavatory if you wanted to get changed for anything, used to carry a towel with you and wipe the sweat out of your eyes halfway through and dump the towel on the side of the stage, and use it when you needed to, and wipe the top of the instruments to get the condensation off. It was all like that, clubs up and down the country were like that, 'cause it was only clubs like that that would have us. The Marquee and then the Flamingo. They were both below ground level and you felt it. You really felt underground in that way and in other ways at that time, 'cause you were doing a certain thing, it was in keeping with the whole thing, but the physical conditions were never good – never.

'Sometimes in those debby gigs we'd get a suite of rooms and a bathroom put at our disposal, which someone in the band would almost immediately defile. Bands always did that sort of thing, they lived up to those traditions. There's always someone who will piss in the sink, and you can't do a thing about it, that's what bands are like. So they got the working conditions . . . or they created the working conditions they were used to – I'm not sure quite which it was, but it was okay 'cause if you wanted to kick the place to pieces you could and you didn't do any damage. There was nothing you could do to most of the places we played.

'The atmosphere at the time, when the Stones did that gig at the Marquee,' Korner said, 'it was tremendously exciting. The feeling of excitement that was generated in the Marquee on Thursday nights with people standing on the tables to see better and sort of – not actually singing with but shouting with and moving with the whole thing – there was a tremendous feeling of something happening, emerging. I think what that particular Thursday, when the Stones played that first gig at the Marquee, did most was to encourage everybody involved into doing it more often. Because people in a Central London club had applauded them as well. At the time, when you're trying to start something, you only need one of those things to convince you that you're going the right way, and then nothing else matters. I think that's what happened with the Stones.

'We lovingly named Keith Mr. Unhealth,' Korner said. 'He always looked like the unhealthiest cat in the group. But we knew he was the strongest physically. Keith was always the first to look really devastated. And once he looked devastated, he'd go for weeks looking no more or less devastated. Meanwhile, the others would slowly deteriorate. But Keith did it rapidly and stayed that way. He really *is* Mr. Unhealth.'

'Brian had gotten an apartment out in the suburbs, Beckenham,' Keith said. 'I started stayin' over with him, virtually livin' there with Brian. Brian has sent the babe and the mother of the babe away. This is also a dodgy situation because there is an awful lot of incestuous relations, like Mick had screwed this chick. So much tension. I'd go over to visit Brian and we'd get into the shit, playin', figuring out Jimmy Reed and such stuff. This was an intense learning period. We would love to make records, but we're not in that league. We wanted to sell records for Jimmy Reed and Muddy Waters and John Lee Hooker and Howlin' Wolf. We were missionaries, disciples, Jesuits. We thought, "If we can turn people on to that, then that's enough." That was the whole total aim . . . the original aim. There was no thought of attaining rock 'n' roll stardom – you had already made the decision to blow that out because if you wanted that then you would have to go through the ballroom route and some promoter, some agent, and you might be given a name like Vince Eager: "As long as you do as we say, you'll look bloody tall – because Moe is not gonna stand for any fucking nonsense my boy, I'm telling you. This is Lou, this is me bruvver Johnny, don't arsk 'is name, 'e's the enforcer." So you immediately wipe yourself out of the mainstream of popular music.

'But at the same time you know something else is going on. You see the excitement that is being created by Alexis, a bunch of old jazzers, old men to us, but the kids are down there watchin' it. They crossed over so quickly, suddenly it wasn't just this university crowd, the kids from the ballrooms were coming into these joints to get onto this stuff. We started to get these weird chick fans, like half Indian, which in London at that time wasn't that common, and some black chicks, and – like teenagers, fifteen, maybe sixteen. These are girls that would normally be waitresses, the type of people you never thought would go for this shit. Brian has to move because he has a fire – it was one of these chicks who started the fire. Mick had found this flat at Edith Grove. Brian moved in with Mick and these other two students from the LSE. Stu's got a job, Mick's on a scholarship from the London School of Economics, Brian gets fired from Whitely's – forced to resign, as in, "If you leave now we won't prosecute." So now Brian has no work at all except the Rolling Stones. To me he's a grown man; two years at that age can be a lifetime almost. I made a few phony attempts at getting jobs, I've done my art school, three years of art school and my dad's working day in and day out and does until retirement day. I've got to go through that too, according to him, so that's the reason I'm in Edith Grove. Either my old dad was gonna put me through the goddamn wall, or – I got out. I knew what I wanted to do was get this band together. At the same time I know that . . . if I wanted to impress my parents, to make something of myself, for bringing me up and feeding me all these years – that I'm not taking the obvious route. I'm going as this very unlikely sort of missionary, but there's nothing I can do about it; that's what Muddy did to me, that's what Chuck and Howlin' Wolf did to me, what they all – Elvis, Buddy, Eddie Cochran, Jerry Lee, Little Richard – all of those cats did to me. They fired me up to the point

37

where it wasn't a matter of conscious decision, it was just – That's what I want to do. I'm only eighteen, already people ain't hearin' this music anymore, and to me, it lit my life up. Now I've got to one way or another keep the flame alive, just for myself. Very selfish. I didn't expect anybody else to think it was that important. When you're that age, you can do that kind of shit. As long as you can survive. But of course once you start living in a place of your own, no matter how mean it is, it's like payin' your own rent makes a man out of you. Every day is a battle for sheer existence.'

CHAPTER 4

Keith was very chubby. He was squat, had fat little legs and wore a little brown hat with little brown boots. He always seemed to have a cold. His nose was always red and his face stark white!

Doris Dupree Richards,
in Barbara Scharone's *Keith Richards*

'So Brian and I are in the middle of London without resources,' Richards said, 'and because of the club thing and the musician thing, we'd often hear about parties, and go to these parties and collect beer bottles, pick up the empties. Drop by, chat, drink a few, when everybody's preoccupied with chicks or whatever, Brian and I would do the room for the deposits on the bottles. If we did enough parties we could pay our rent just from beer bottles. For food we used to hit the supermarkets, a tomato here, a potato there . . . and we never got done. I never considered myself an expert shoplifter but I mean, we did all right.

'We had been doing it for I guess the best part of a year, putting the Stones together, not playing any gigs but just rehearsing. Sometimes Alexis would let us do three or four numbers in intervals. I don't suppose he was particularly enthusiastic, but since he was the guy that brought us all together and we used to call on Alexis for advice, in a way it was like his paternal responsibility to give us a break now and again. We'd do three or four of Muddy's numbers, a Jimmy Reed song. Immediately, it became fairly clear that there was a lot of interest in those interval spots. Giorgio Gomelsky, who's Russian, managed a club called the

41

Crawdaddy, down on the Thames in Richmond. He heard us a couple of times and gave us a weekly gig.'

Giorgio Gomelsky, when last heard of, was in Manhattan, 'still doing the same thing,' Keith said, 'spotting people and trying to put them together. He liked our band. With Giorgio suddenly the Stones had somebody who knew the club game, the club scene of London and had been dealing with it for many years. He had a typewriter and everything. God knows how these guys made an existence. London was a big enough town to support its own sort of subterranean culture. If you were on top of it, you could do a few articles for the *New Spectator*, a BBC script here and there. Alexis would do voice-overs. Had that wonderfully rich voice. You could hear him selling yogurt.' Keith would not deny that early on he himself, with the Stones, did a London radio commercial for Rice Krispies, the cereal that went 'Snap . . . Crackle . . . Pop.'

Another figure who would affect the Stones' career was Londoner Andrew Loog Oldham, a twenty-year-old mod-rocker who affected a persona which might have come from *A Clockwork Orange*. 'Andrew had been working for [Brian] Epstein, the Beatles' manager, doing PR,' Keith said. 'He'd seen the way the Beatles had taken off. He was there at the instigation of it and had been involved in that whole explosion of the Beatles. Even though they've only had two hits, by now everybody knows a whole new thing is happening. After "Love Me Do" everybody knew, "This thing's changed."

'These things happened so quickly – the word's around that this band's starting to kick up quite a bit of a stink around the West London area, a regular gig at the Crawdaddy and a couple on the Eel Pie Island – there's like three hundred people on the inside, and a thousand on the outside can't get in.'

In the United Kingdom during the early post-Second World War era, work permits were extremely difficult for foreigners to obtain. Those for recording artists or enter tainers were restricted to unique individuals. It didn't suffice just to be an American Federation of Musicians trumpet player; you had to be Louis Armstrong. While this kept out many worthy American artists, it led to the practice of, say at the Watford Gaumont cinema, Reg Thorpe appearing as Fats Domino. An Englishman would come onstage, sit at a piano and do Fats Domino's act. By the mid-fifties the work restrictions had been relaxed, but in the sixties the idea of vernacular American-style music being produced by Eng lishmen was quite new for them even as interpreters, much less as composers.

Still, it was happening. Because there was no phone any- where near the Edith Grove flat, the Stones advertised their gigs using Stu's telephone number at his employers', Imperial Chemical Industries. Andrew Oldham called Stu, who sent him round to see the others; they invited him to come to one of their Crawdaddy gigs.

'I'd never seen anything like it,' Oldham said later. 'You *know* when you're in a room with a fanatical audience. I was quite overpowered and a little taken aback. If I hadn't made any plans before, that evening I definitely knew what I wanted to do. It was very apparent that I wanted to manage them. It seemed like what I was *meant* to do.'

'Andrew sees immediately,' Keith said, 'that there's room for more than one act. He was looking for an alternative to the Beatles because he couldn't work for them anymore. I guess Andrew's mind would work this way: If Liverpool can produce the Beatles, what can London produce? Liverpool was much further away from London than it is now. There were no streets, no highways. I mean, Liverpool is . . . as far as London is concerned, it's like Nome, Alaska. To a guy that's been brought up in London, it's like you'd rather go to France than go north of Watford . . . especially at that time.

'Andrew had a gig with Eric Easton. He was the PR. Easton

had been in show business all his life. He was a musician who'd learnt all the tricks of vaudeville, the insides and outsides of the English music and theatre business, this old pier organist who was now managing a couple of top acts. He's got a business going, he's not a big-time guy, but he's got acts hitting the Top Ten. He knows the mechanics of the bookings. He knows more than anybody because he's spent thirty years looking for a booking. And in the process he's found out how it's done and he's better off booking other people than himself.

'What intrigued one about Easton was Andrew. Andrew wanted to be Phil Spector overnight. And the minute Andrew made some bread off the Stones it was the Chevrolet – and in England you didn't see many a Chevy convertible, metallic blue – with some hard guy called Reg, the driver. Andrew would sit beside him and say, "Go for it, Reg!" There would be like three fucking trucks coming down the tube at you and – "Reg, hit the fucking tube, slide job" – almost suicidal glee in making it.'

Under Easton and Oldham's management, the Stones signed a recording contract with London's Decca Records. On May 10, 1963, at their first professional recording session, they cut two songs for their first single release: a Chuck Berry song called 'Come On,' and Chicago songwriter Willie Dixon's 'I Wanna Be Loved.' Andrew had asked for their five most commercial songs, and these two were among them. 'Come On' was a justly obscure Chuck Berry effort; 'I Wanna Be Loved' failed to deliver the Stones' hard-edged Muddy Waters sound. Both songs were lighter than the Stones in live performance, and the band drove Andrew 'absolutely potty,' Stu said, by refusing to play 'Come On' once it had been released.

'At the end of that first recording session,' Oldham said,

'I went, "Hmmm, right, let's go." And the engineer said to me, "What about mixing it?" I said, "What's that?" and he looked at me like, "What the fuck is this?" I think he tried to be as nice about it as possible. Everybody in the group was just as interested to hear what mixing was. He said, "We have four tracks, and in order for it to become a record, we have to get it down to one." I said, "Oh, you do that, I'll come back in the morning," thinking that if I stay it will probably take longer, and time is money.'

Decca executives insisted on the Stones' recutting the two sides at Decca's West Hampstead studios, but the record was at last released, on June 7, to hang around the middle of the English Top Fifty charts for over three months. They performed the A-side, 'Come On,' at the Birmingham studio of the pop-music television show, 'Thank Your Lucky Stars.' They wore a band uniform consisting of dark slacks and neckties and black-and-white houndstooth-check jackets. They had no piano player. Andrew, seeing Mick Jagger as a potential sex symbol – somebody said that on his first visit to the Crawdaddy, 'he looked at Jagger as Sylvester looks at Tweetie Pie' – and the conventionally groomed and attired Ian Stewart as anomalous to his perception of what should be the group's image, insisted that Brian put Stu out of the band, which Brian acquiesced in doing. 'Brian had to blow Stu out,' Keith said, 'because Andrew Oldham said six guys is too many. And there's Stu in his charcoal-gray suit from the office and his tie on. Bless his sweet soul. It came to the point that he created a whole new fashion genre, the corduroy jeans with the wallet and screwdriver in the bulging back pocket and the moccasins. To Stu clothes were something you have to feel comfortable in and that was the only criterion.'

Stu's decision to stay as the band's roadie was, as Keith later called it, 'incredibly big-hearted.' I played Stu the tape of Keith saying that about him, and Stu was very touched, so much so that he said, 'Oh, bollocks,' or words to that effect. 'I figured I could still enjoy what I was doing and stay around. But you have to be a little bitter. After all, it wasn't nicely done. But this isn't a very nice business.'

The second half of 1963 saw the Stones playing almost every night at some (in Stu's phrase) 'terribly thick place like Wisbech or Cambridge.'

About the time their record dropped from the charts, the Stones changed their living arrangements – Mick and Keith moving into a flat with Andrew, Brian moving in with Linda Lawrence, a girl he'd met in Windsor, and her parents. Also around this time, Andrew happened to run into Beatles John Lennon and Paul McCartney, who gave the Stones a song that became the Stones' next release, 'I Wanna Be Your Man.' The most remarkable thing about the record is an eight-bar guitar break by Brian Jones that sounds not at all like anything recorded previously by any European, except possibly the Gypsy guitarist Django Reinhardt. Also notable is Nanker Phelge, author of the B-side titled 'Stoned,' based on the chord structure of the MG's 'Green Onions,' with Stu playing celestial honky-tonk barrelhouse piano. It was an in-joke, but not entirely. A 'nanker' was a particular kind of ugly face; 'pulling a nanker' involved pushing up the nose and pulling down the under-eye sockets, good for confronting newspaper photographers. Phelge, who wasn't named that but insisted on being called it, lived with Keith, Mick, and Brian at Edith Grove. 'Absolutely the most disgusting human being you ever met,' Keith said; 'also the most lovable. He was the only one who wasn't part of this band, so he kind of roadied for us a bit and brought our spirits up . . . He also created a lot of trouble. He was the sort of guy that – you'd open the front door and he'd be standing there, streaked, skidmarked underpants on his head, totally naked. "How ya doin', boys?" A hidden hero.' It didn't matter what name the Stones used for writing credit since they were all in it together. Or so it seemed at the time.

The Stones had finished doing club dates – they wouldn't do another one for years – the week before starting their first tour of English cinemas. Also on the bill were Bo Diddley, Little Richard, and the Everly Brothers. Watching their heroes every night, Keith said later, was what drew them into the pop side of the music business. Bo Diddley would never forget the Stones, and the spectacle of a blond, black-eyed [Keith had punched him] Brian Jones, backstage playing Bo's song 'Mona' fit to raise the dead. Brian got punched because he interfered with Keith's carefully laid – no pun intended – plans. Keith was sleeping at this time with a girl named Linda Keith, daughter of a London disc jockey. Knowing how much time there was until the show and how hungry he'd be after fucking Linda, Keith carefully provided for himself in the dressing room a box of fried chicken. Except for Brian – as they were going from the dressing room to the stage, Keith served sentence: 'You cunt, you et me chicken.'

The Stones were glad at the time to stop playing clubs. The driving had been insane. 'When we decided to go on the road,' Keith said, 'the M1 had just about made it to Birmingham; that was the first four-lane, barrier down the middle, real highway. Otherwise it could take all day to get up somewhere around Liverpool instead of three or four hours, so it was a much bigger country in terms of getting about it. The hardest thing in England ever to do and probably still not easy, is to go east to west. Everything goes north and south and you've got to find your own way. We did gigs where you'd go from the farthest east place in the country to the farthest west, along little two-lane paths.'

Less than a week into 1964, the Stones toured England with the Ronettes. Their lead singer, Veronica Bennett, would become Mrs. Phil Spector. As he had with the Beatles, Oldham did free PR for Spector, America's then reigning rock 'n' roll production genius. So it happened that Spector, who came to England in February, was present at the recording session for the Stones' third single. 'I Wanna Be Your Man' had been an English Top Ten hit, making it to number nine. Andrew said that the choice of the third single came about at the flat where he, Mick, and Keith were living. 'We'd just been sitting around and wondering what to do next,' he said. 'We were all sitting there singing a whole lot of Buddy Holly songs. Keith had this twelve-string guitar and did a shortened version of "Not Fade Away." He'd hardly done more than a few bars when it struck us all together. Phil Spector came in on the session and played maracas. Actually, he and Mick wrote the B-side, "Little by Little." '

Spector and Jagger had huddled in the hallway for a few minutes, long enough to devise a Nanker Phelge/Spector lost-love/car song with lines stolen from blues singers like Robert Wilkins: 'Things ain't been the same, since my mother died.' It earned Spector a writer's credit and some money. He held on to the rights, too, indicating that he really was a genius.

'Not Fade Away,' with its Buddy Holly changes and Bo Diddley rhythms, was a perfect Stones vehicle. The band's track of 'Little by Little' made up for the song's scarce lyrics with fervent harmonica and scorching guitar interplay, on a bed of Charlie Watts. The record was the first by the Stones to make it into the American charts. It hit the *Cashbox* Hot 100 at number ninety-eight. The Stones' eponymously titled first album, consisting mainly of songs associated with their heroes Bo Diddley, Slim Harpo, Chuck Berry, Rufus Thomas, Jimmy Reed, and Muddy Waters, had been released. The liner notes, by Andrew Oldham, said, 'They have emerged as five well-rounded intelligent talents, who will journey successfully far beyond the realms of pop music.' From the beginning there was an expectation of transcendence, a need to make of what had been recreation something more – as Andrew said, 'a way of life.' On June 1 the Rolling Stones left England for their first tour of the United States.

'It was obvious,' Keith said, 'that Easton had booked us into impossible gigs, that this guy, outside of Blackpool, anywhere beyond the shores of England, this cat was lost. I remember Omaha ... about sixty people in a fifteen-thousand-seat auditorium. The edges were great – in San Bernardino, L.A. Swing Auditorium, New York, Chicago, too, we did very well, but the communications then were far slower than they have become. You didn't have MTV to spread you overnight, straight through twenty-four hours a day. But the "beautiful people" discovered us, which is very similar to what happened in London, the weird deb thing we did, the height of fascination with the low-life creature. We always attracted them.

'We came back in October of the same year and still played to some empty places, and probably early the next year, too, a lot of empty ... After "Satisfaction" everywhere was full, if you were working the edges of big towns they would be rocking, but before that ... The thing is, those empty towns, that's where you learn your craft, how to put on a show when there's like ten people in a place that seats a thousand. Or a hundred people in a place that seats five thousand and you play to these few and the joint's rocking still. And everybody has forgotten about all of these empty seats, this vast cavern that we can see as we're looking at them, and they're just looking at you and to them the room is that small. So you manage to create this whole new environment – we're looking at this huge cavern of empty seats, it looks like a wedding party down front. You don't give them a chance to look over their shoulder. You say, "If I can do this, if I can stop these people from looking over their shoulders and realizing that it's not a happening event..." To us, just to get the chance to come to America, to us that was already a bigger payoff than we ever expected. Let alone having people come to see you play. Anybody in the Stones who tells you about it is not really reliable as information. To us, just to get there – America was fairyland. It had all the hits, all the music, and... nobody in their lives had a way of getting there once just for a visit. Forget it, no way. To be paid to go there and play to Americans, we're shitting ourselves. At the same time, we've got a certain confidence because suddenly a gig to us is chicks screaming at us.

'This is where Andrew comes back into the picture. Once the first album has taken off – writing songs, that's what mystifies us. The Beatles, they're writing their own shit. We're not like that. We interpret...

'I'm a guitar player. To me a songwriter is... you want a plumber when the water fucks up, and if your horse loses a shoe you want a blacksmith, they're that far apart... Now I know that everybody is a songwriter and it's just a matter of whether they put it together or not. Andrew saw very quickly after the first album, he said, "Look, either we've gotta find somebody to write songs and then lock them up and keep them to ourselves or... whaddya gonna do? Just some more cover versions. There's a few out there. You can do it for another album or two and still... without a source of new material... write some songs together." And I'm saying, "That's not my job." So... virtually, what he did was lock us up in the kitchen for a night and say, "Don't come out without a song." So we sat around and came up with "As Tears Go By," the most unlikely Rolling Stones material, but that's what happens when you write songs, you immediately fly to some other realm... I can't connect it with what I'm doing. Of course the weird thing is that he found Marianne Faithfull at the same time and bunged it onto her, and it was a fucking hit, so already we're songwriters. But it took us a few months, rest of that year, to dare to write anything for the Stones.

'Before "The Last Time," songwriting to me was just an irksome practice that I saw the point of since we got a hit with the first one, but it was always for Andrew's peripheral things that he had going on his own. And then we had the hit with Gene Pitney, "That Girl Belongs to Yesterday." We were already writing hit songs but like on the side. No way we would touch these things with a barge pole by ourselves. Trying to get around to writing one we could record took quite a while, but once we got into realizing that, "Hey, we already had a couple of hits," we thought, "All we got to do is work on it, and we probably will find it." And so we started to work toward that end. "The Last Time" quite honestly is an old gospel song the Staple Singers did, PD. I just rearranged it.

'There's only one song anyway. Everything's just a variation.'

'Mediocre composers borrow,' Stravinsky said. 'Great composers steal.'

'At the Hilton in London,' Keith recalled, 'just there for a night or two – something to do with Allen Klein and a record deal we were doing – I woke up in the middle of the night and I dreamt this riff. Which I don't do that often. That was the first time that had ever happened to me. Because I'm on the road, just passing through London, happens to be my town but I'm only there for a night and so I've got my guitar, the early Phillips cassette player, the first one, the role model, and I just picked up the guitar and... "*I can't get no satisfaction... I can't get no satisfaction*"... *snore*... The only way I found it again was the next morning I look and, checking out my gear, the recorder was set at the start, ready to roll. I look at it and it's gone all the way through. I don't remember anything about this. How did that happen? Who pushed the button? Somebody came in during the night and has put some message on it. Mick or one of the boys, they got into the room and said, "Fuck you, Keith Richards, piece of shit..." I want to find out what's happened to this cassette, how it's gotten from start to finish, and there's like

51

thirty seconds of "Satisfaction" and sixty minutes of me snoring. I realize that I can snore occasionally.

'We weren't about to let this music go down the tube. What turned us on was Elvis and Little Richard and Chuck Berry and Bo Diddley and Eddie Cochran and Buddy Holly – we're rock 'n' roll freaks, basically, except we've felt we missed out on some grounding. And so we went back to sort of research and find out where the hell the music came from. I had heard plenty of blues in my time but not played like that, not raw, the blues I heard would be . . . if Count Basie played the blues, all arranged, already a big complicated deal. It wasn't like just three or four guys out where the Count got it from. We wanted to know where it came from. You still have a very huge and lively interest in England in soul music and black music. You don't get "Blue Suede Shoes" from nowhere. Nothing comes out of nowhere. These cats been listening to some shit, whether they know it or not, that has produced this. Then you start to realize that music is the most subtle thing in the world for conveying ideas.'

CHAPTER 5

Rainer Maria Rilke . . . said that fame was the coming together of misconceptions and rumors about a new name.

Michael Mott

'**B**rian was this weird kind of guy,' Keith said. 'He had to create a sort of schism. He needed some sort of conspiracy feeling to his life. Mick and him against me, or whatever, which is fine when you've got plenty of time. You can deal with it. But on the road when everybody's working, tryin' to make the next gig – it was an exhausting day for four or five years, working 340-odd gigs a year.

'The first alienation came when Mick and I started writing. I realized that I was becoming very much like Brian. Mick and I were being merciless on him, because you don't have the patience at the time, when you're working that hard, to take it. So you would start to become vicious and that was the same thing that Brian would have done, had done at times himself. Stu hated Brian's guts. The more he got to know him, the more he hated him. Brian was, as Stu said, a very difficult person. The harder the work got, the more awkward he got . . . and then the more fucked up he would get himself when he didn't get his way, until we would be working three weeks in the Midwest with one guitar player, namely me. Which is where I learned what the Rolling Stones were all about. You can't cover what you want from the Stones with one guitar.'

'There's two ways of looking at it,' Stu said. 'You can say Brian formed the group or you can say if Brian never existed Mick and Keith would have formed a group that sounded pretty much like the Rolling Stones. Chronologically, Brian did form the group. But Mick, Keith and Dick Taylor would have done it anyway. In a lot of respects Brian was very little help musically. Brian worked at being a rebel. Keith was born a rebel.'

◙

Superficially, Brian and Mick had more in common than Mick and Keith. Both Brian and Mick were a bit above working class in their backgrounds. Mick's mother sold Royal Beauty Products, the English equivalent of Avon, but Mick's father was an educator of sorts, even if the education was physical. Brian's father worked for Rolls-Royce, and his mother gave piano lessons. Brian was the only one of the Stones to receive a really proper musical education, though Bill Perks, who (changing his last name to Wyman) became the Rolling Stones' bass player, had taken lessons – learning piano, organ, and clarinet in his early teens.

What Brian and Keith had in common was months of rehearsing while Brian learned how to play harmonica and they learned to play together every song they knew by the masters – Jimmy Reed, Bo Diddley, Muddy Waters, Slim Harpo, Howlin' Wolf, Chuck Berry, and so on. 'With gloves on, freezing my balls off,' Keith said. 'That's the closest I ever got to Brian Jones, at that point where we dissected this stuff.' The nights of playing four or five hours in pubs allowed the virus of the boogie disease to have its way with the two young musicians. Even Stu, by no means Brian's greatest fan, said that Keith and Brian played together not like two guitarists but like one guitarist's two hands.

◙

America taught the Stones new lessons of many kinds. They recorded sixteen songs at Chess Studios in Chicago, where so many of their favorite records came from. Muddy Waters was there and touched their hearts with his gracious humility; he helped them carry in their equipment. Even Chuck Berry, who'd snubbed them in England, welcomed them to Chess. They'd just done a TV show in California with Dean Martin, Frank Sinatra's buddy, who showed no mercy in ridiculing them. Then Chuck Berry acts like Mr. Nice Guy. And a couple of days after that, in Omaha, where the public auditorium the Stones played prohibited alcohol, a cop came into the Stones' dressing room, saw a bottle of scotch, and pulled a gun on Keith, forcing him to pour a plain Coca-Cola down a toilet. The next day Keith bought a .38 revolver like the one the cop had, so he'd be equal. America the beautiful.

Back in England, the Stones' next single, cut at Chess – Bobby and Shirley Womack's 'It's All Over Now,' previously a small hit for the Valentinos on Sam Cooke's SAR label – became the Stones' first number one. 'We used to go down to the local record stores,' Keith said, 'buy up a whole bunch of soul singles, sit down by the record player and learn 'em. Then we'd do 'em as quickly as possible.' The B-side, 'Good Times, Bad Times,' was by two writers named Mick Jagger and Keith Richards. Nanker Phelge had to split royalties five ways; this made it fifty-fifty. The song was a slow blueslike ballad – melodic, pleasant, giving little indication of what was to come. (While in the U.S. the Stones had released a single for that market. 'Tell Me,' by Keith and Mick, was their first A-side. It was backed with another Willie Dixon song associated with Muddy, 'I Just Want to Make Love to You.' They would release another U.S. single, Norman Meade's 'Time Is On my Side' and the Jagger-Richards composition, 'Congratulations,' while trying to find something strong enough to follow their number-one domestic hit, 'It's All Over Now.') Keeping the momentum going at home, they immediately returned to the road, playing the larger concert halls. Brian, a continuing problem, managed to get left onstage and nearly pulled to pieces by frenetic fans at the Queen's Hall in Leeds. By now he and Linda Lawrence had a child, Brian's third son. Brian kept threatening to marry her, but never did.

A few days after the Leeds concert, Keith nearly kicked a goon who was spitting at him in Blackpool, causing a riot and the immediate utter destruction of that hall, including the grand piano and Charlie's borrowed drums. The Stones barely got away from the place with their lives. A career in music was first of all an education in survival.

Brian had missed English dates almost from the beginning, but once the Stones had the slightest shred of hope for success in the U.S., the ante was much higher, and there was as a result less slack. When in October they returned to the U.S., Brian collapsed from some ailment and Keith learned hard lessons about trying to get the music to work with half the guitar parts missing. That very nearly did it for Brian; the band had a mind to kick him out, but by the time they played Chicago he made a heroic recovery, and they went on together.

Keith and Mick were still struggling with their inability to write Rolling Stones songs; at the end of 1964, desperate for an English release, the band put out another Willie Dixon song, this one more closely associated with Howlin' Wolf – 'Little Red Rooster.' (Though Sam Cooke did a sort of Harry Belafonte meets Bill Doggett version, far whiter than the Stones'.) Brian plays some highly effective bottleneck. 'At that time,' Keith said, 'releasing "Little Red Rooster" was our distinction. The only way we could set ourselves apart from everything else that was going on.' The B-side, the Jagger-Richards song 'Off the Hook,' reused the "fraid of what I'd find' line from 'Little by Little' – Mick recycling before it became the fashion. Roy Carr called it 'a great mid-tempo garage band song with a shuffle beat and one of many Jagger-Richards compositions concerned with hard-as-nails teen queens.' They released another just-for-America single, two more Jagger-Richards originals: 'Heart of Stone' and 'What a Shame.' They were on the verge of something.

By February of the next year Keith had made a break-through; on the way to their first tour of Australia, they stopped off in Los Angeles to record 'The Last Time.'

'There's no point,' Keith told *Guitar Player*, 'in writing songs on a sheet of paper, going verse, chorus, verse, chorus, and regarding this as a song. No, it ain't. A song is music, and I'd rather start with the music and then get into the attitude of the track and put something on top of it. I never sit down and say, "Time to write a song. Now I'm going to write." To me, that would be fatal. To me the important thing is recognizing something when it comes by.'

But the records they had cut, even in America, were too rushed in every aspect – preparation, performance, mixing, mastering – to begin to capture the excitement of the Stones playing live. 'We all knew,' Keith said, 'that the sound we were getting live and in the studio was not what we were getting on record – the difference was light-years apart.'

The patterns of road behavior at this point were: Charlie disoriented and homesick for his wife Shirley; Brian and Bill competing to see which one could get the most girls; Mick and Keith writing songs. Nobody drank too much or took drugs; the pace, as Keith later noted, wouldn't permit it. Returning from Australia to England, they embarked on their fifth British tour, which included one of their most absurd legendary scenes, Wyman, Jones and Jagger being arrested for peeing in the open (at a garage in Stratford whose manager wouldn't let them use the toilet). They toured Scandinavia, played a *New Musical Express* pollwinner's tour at Wembley Stadium, and on April 13 played the Olympia Theatre in Paris, where they met a girl backstage – a North Italian fashion model named Anita Pallenberg.

Then – *zip* – back to the U.S. for their third tour. Sitting around the pool at a motel in Clearwater, Florida, Keith and Mick worked on the song that had come to Keith in his sleep at the London Hilton; a few days later, in Los Angeles, the Stones would record it. 'I was screaming for more distortion: "This riff's really gotta hang hard and long," ' Keith told guitar maven Jas Obrecht. 'We burnt the amps up and turned the shit up, and it still wasn't right. And then Ian Stewart went around the corner to Wallach's Music City or something and came around with a distortion box: "Try this." ' Keith didn't like the record; he thought it would be a flop; his stomach was filled with the butterflies of anxiety.

Released in June, 'Satisfaction' – in spite of its being, as Robert Palmer has pointed out, 'a quasi-Marxist critique of consumerism and its cost to society, and to the individual, disguised as a mindlessly sexy rock 'n' roll song' – would become, to many, the archetypal rock 'n' roll song.

A lot of people, though, thought Keith and Mick hit their writing stride with the two B-sides to 'Satisfaction' – 'Under Assistant West Coast Promotion Man' and 'The Spider and the Fly' (the first for the U.S., second for the U.K.) – satirical contemporary portraits worthy of an r&b Daumier. Who could forget the former's 'seersucker suit' or that the latter 'was common, flirty; she looked about thirty.'

By this time the Beatles had released two feature movies, *A Hard Day's Night* and *Help!,* and even the more esoteric Bob Dylan had starred in a grainy and authentic documentary film titled *Don't Look Back.* Thinking that the same fate, film stardom, awaited them, the Stones made management adjustments, awarding Eric Easton a golden handshake and the key to the highway. Andrew Oldham brought in a new comanager, an American named Allen Klein, a New York Jewish kid who'd grown up the hard way and become a C.P.A., working for entertainers, doing audits of record companies that never failed to owe their artists. Klein had eventually managed Sam Cooke, until Cooke's untimely demise. An audacious accountant, Klein would wind up owning extensive rights to the amazing body of songs written by the Stones in the 1960s – most of Keith and Mick's best work.

In September, the Stones, back in Los Angeles at RCA Studios, where Sam Cooke had recorded, cut the next single, based on the 'Twist and Shout' changes – with an extra chord in the chorus: 'Get Off My Cloud,' another astonishing explosion of complaint; raucous, intelligent, energetic, good-humored complaint. That same month, the Stones did a tour of five German cities. Violent scenes occurred with mounted police; crowds of fans were dispersed with hoses and clubs.

'Satisfaction' was number one in *Billboard* for the second week on September 15, when they played Munich. The girl they'd met in Paris, Anita Pallenberg, was there and spent the night with Brian, who spent the night crying because Keith and Mick had hurt his feelings.

'Brian and I were at odds for years,' Richards said. "Sixty-five through 'sixty-six. He'd been playing Mick and me against each other. He was a manipulator, something you don't need when you're working that many days a year – "You got ten days off? Make an album." That was a vacation. Then he turns up with Anita and – I still have to check myself today on whether I decided to become friends with Brian again so's to ingratiate myself with her. I'm bein' honest, I'm tryna figure out . . . I think it's fifty-fifty. As fascinating as Anita was, she scared the pants off me. She knew everything and she could say it in five languages. At the time, I was concerned with Brian; I found myself hanging with Brian again and he kind of appreciated it. But I don't know if he appreciated that he could use it against Mick – I don't know how much of it was his thing about playing one

61

person up against another. Which he did automatically, no matter who he was involved with and no matter what situation.'

A year elapsed between the reemergence of Anita and Keith's refound friendship with Brian. Anita kept turning up, meeting Brian in Miami during the Stones' fourth U.S. tour, and after the tour in Los Angeles, where the Stones went to record *Aftermath*, their first album consisting entirely of original songs by Keith and Mick. Brian, father of three, told the press that Anita was the first girl he'd ever been serious about. Hot dark eyes, a good, slightly uptilted nose, lean gorgeous legs, large dark aureoles and perky nipples, a wicked sexual quality and an unexpected intelligence, acquaintance with New York poets like Frank O'Hara and *Vogue* models, and a sure aesthetic sense made Anita truly formidable. Not for no reason was she cast as the black witch in *Barbarella*.

CHAPTER 6

My idol is Keith Richards, the Rolling Stones rhythm guitarist who made menacing music out of the Dionysian darkness . . .

Camille Paglia

Everything that the Stones had expected had turned out to be false; the music they loved had a vastly wider audience and greater significance than any of them could have foreseen in his maddest imaginings. The tour they had just completed, less than six weeks of work, made them two million dollars. The next record, released in November 1965 in the U.S. and on the heels of January in the U.K., was a remake of 'As Tears Go By,' arranged by Keith and Mike Leander, who'd arranged Marianne Faithfull's original 1964 hit recording of the song. Like 'Satisfaction' and 'Get Off My Cloud' – though unlike them in almost every other way – it went straight to number one. It was followed, early in February 1966, by '19th Nervous Breakdown,' which attained a kind of perfect match of notes to syllables that rivals the constructions of a Stephen Foster or a Johnny Mercer, but few would see that skill because of the content.

Bob Dylan wrote about a girl with 'her fog, her amphetamine, and her pearls,' and people said he was a poet. The Beatles had been revealed, proclaimed, as art. But neither Dylan nor the Beatles made records as hard, as uncompromisingly physical – 'shake your arse' music – as the Stones, who were therefore less easily acceptable to the general public, as if such a thing existed. As their music deepened, Keith and Mick would receive many royalty checks but little serious critical respect. It wasn't surprising; few music critics in England or America were knowledgeable in the areas of blues and rhythm & blues, wherein lay the roots of the Stones' music. Other musicians knew how good it was. Leonard Bernstein called their next single, 'Paint It Black,' one of the greatest compositions of the twentieth century. It would be the Stones' sixth straight number one in England.

On that record, as on many others, Brian Jones provided unique instrumental assistance. For 'Paint It Black,' he spent hours sitting in the studio learning sitar, put it on the record, and never played it again. 'Brian had this power of concentration,' Keith said. 'He could pick up an instrument he's never played before and in an hour or so he'd have it figured out.'

The barometer of success, though, was Keith. Dave Hassinger, who engineered their early Los Angeles recordings, said, 'You knew if it was a good take by Keith's smile. I always remember looking at Keith and if he was smiling we had a good take. Keith never said anything. He just smiled. And it would never be questioned, never a discussion. Honest to God, I could never tell by Mick's expression or Andrew's at the end of a take but I could tell by Keith's smile. It was *there*. Nothing was accepted unless Keith smiled. And that was it.'

Because of the Stones, the Beatles and the Yardbirds and Animals and Who and Kinks, and such things as James Bond novels and new English film stars and directors, London in the spring of 1966 was the most fashionable town on earth. Keith and Mick had been photographed by the photographer of the royals, Cecil Beaton – 'poor, bald Beaton,' Lady Diana

Cooper called him – who said she behaved like a brunette, and compared the young rockers to Renaissance angels.

By the spring of 1966, the Stones' pace had slackened just a bit. Keith found time to buy, but not live in, Redlands, a thatch-roofed country house with a moat, near the village of West Wittering in Sussex. In June, *Aftermath* was released, and the Stones went back to the U.S. Thanks to the composing genius of Keith and Mick, the album was filled with not simply performances, but characteristic Stones compositions, like 'High and Dry.' That song, '19th Nervous Breakdown,' and 'Connection,' among others, indicated a development that would prove most significant to Keith. Like Dylan and the Beatles and many other young people in and out of show business, Keith had been getting into something that was, to some people at the time, a sacrament – the sacrament of dope.

'We were actually trying to do something by taking a few chemicals and making this wrench,' Keith said. 'It comes down to mundane things like hair and clothes and music, but the ideal behind it was very pure. Everybody at that point was prepared to use himself as a sort of laboratory, to find some way out of this mess. It was very idealistic and very destructive at the same time for a lot of people. But the downside of it now is that people think that drugs are entertainment. They don't know that the cats they look up to who died of drugs – and even me, who was supposed to but didn't – yet – we weren't takin' drugs just for fun, recreation. Creation, maybe.'

The Stones' fifth tour of the U.S. started in June. They played sold-out stadiums, but they weren't popular with everybody. The United States' involvement in military hostilities in Vietnam was growing, and people felt warlike. In Syracuse, Brian snatched a large American flag that had been spread out backstage to dry, and a stagehand snatched it back.

Even unaided by a pugnacious atmosphere, Brian provoked hostility; at the end of the tour they cut the new single
and tracks for their next album in Los Angeles, then went
on separate holidays. Brian and Anita were in Morocco,
where they had a fight and Brian hit Anita, breaking his
hand. Luckily, 'Have You Seen Your Mother, Baby, Standing
in the Shadow?' was already in the can. Its picture sleeve,
presenting the Stones in drag, would become justly famous.
'Ain't no doubt about it,' London music writer Roy Carr
said, 'since the release of "The Last Time," the first thing
that attracted the listener to every new Stones record was
the noise. "Have You Seen Your Mother, Baby, Standing in
the Shadow?" galvanized everything they'd recorded since,
into a taped bacchanalia of excess.' Which may be a polite
way of saying it was overproduced. Keith contends that the
record was great, but hasty mixing and mastering because
of Decca's greedy impatience to get the product out buried
the rhythm section and didn't do the song justice. CD technology certainly improves the sound, no doubt about that,
but those horn parts ain't by Arif Mardin, baby. The best
thing about that release was the B-side, a driving bluesy
throwback to sweaty nights in clubs, called 'Who's Driving
Your Plane,' one of the all-time greatest Stones tracks, Stu
outstanding throughout. As it turned out, Stu couldn't be
fired. The record was released in September, by which time
Keith was living with Brian and Anita at their flat in Courtfield Road.

That flat, where Keith, Brian, and Anita lived, was the
absolute center of swinging London. The best drugs, the best
music, the most interesting young creative types, all came to
the Jones-Richards-Pallenberg *salon*. In the blink of an eye –
between 1964 and, well, it would soon be 1967 – a revolution

had occurred among young people, a stylistic change in fashions, hairstyles, and music. Everywhere you saw men and boys with longer hair; it crept downward, caressing and then enveloping ears and shirt collars. At the time, for the length of that historical moment, it seemed you could look at people and know what music they listened to, books they read, drugs they did.

In late September, the Stones toured England, playing places like the Albert Hall with the Yardbirds (who'd studied their craft at the Stones' feet at the Crawdaddy week after week before taking over the Stones' gig there) and Ike and Tina Turner. The year seemed to end quietly, but the silence turned out to be foreboding.

The first ruckus of the new year for Keith and the Stones took place in New York City, where the Stones went to perform their new single on the popular 'Ed Sullivan' TV show. Good Catholic Ed refused, however, to allow Mick to sing the title line of the song 'Let's Spend the Night Together.' Sullivan, that tasteful lyricist, insisted the words 'the night' be changed to 'some time.' For a couple of days New York radio stations carried reports the Stones might refuse to do the show, but at last they did it, with Mick saying neither phrase, just garbling the words. 'Together' was a classic disco record, released years before the genre existed. Ironically, the B-side, Keith's composition 'Ruby Tuesday,' would go to number one, the Stones' first in the U.S. since 'Satisfaction.' Brian played flute on the record; it was, Stu observed, the last thing he ever did for the Stones. That wasn't true – Brian played mellotron on 'We Love You' and brilliant guitar on *Beggar's Banquet* – but it was one of the last such instrumental specialty performances from Brian, who also recorded on guitars, saxophone, harmonica, organ, marimba, sitar, dulcimer, recorder, bells, and harpsichord. 'Dying all the time,'

69

Keith wrote in 'Ruby Tuesday'; 'Lose your dreams and you will lose your mind.'

◉

The counterpart in England of the Sullivan production was 'The London Palladium Show', another vaudeville-based enterprise aimed at the vast wasteland of ordinary folk. The Stones had avoided the show in the past, and it was seen as significant that they had contracted to appear there. 'Have You Seen Your Mother, Baby' had made it no higher than number five, and journalists wondered whether the pop craze might be ending, the Stones forced to seek more traditional audiences.

As it turned out, Keith and Brian violated all sorts of Palladium traditions. First, they showed up for rehearsal hours late and full of LSD; Brian insisted on blatantly displaying a large hookah atop a piano. The Stones, knowing what TV sound engineers were like, violated a ban on broadcasting taped music by bringing along a backing track; but all these offenses were unimportant compared to the roundabout. To an outsider it seems meaningless, but to the Palladium, to the people of Great Britain, the roundabout was tradition – actually, the Palladium's stage, which revolved; the show's acts ended each week's production by waving and throwing kisses to the folks at home. Waving and throwing kisses not being their style, the Stones refused to revolve. Hard to believe the size of the insult – it was as if the Stones had insulted every family watching the show, as if they'd gone into these people's homes and offended them. The whole thing threw a major wrench into the Stones' ties with Andrew Oldham, who walked out on the show, declaring himself no part of the Stones' actions. In retrospect it might appear a major incident in the Stones' past had real disaster not been only a few days away.

Two weeks later, Mick was on a London radio talk show

denying a report in the tabloid *News of the World* that he, among other pop stars, had taken LSD. Mick promised to sue, and two days later had the paper served with a writ for libel. This trouble had come about because Brian had been babbling in Blaise's. A *News of the World* reporter in the hip King's Road *boîte* observed Brian Jones taking pills and showing some girls a chunk of hashish, inviting them to his house for a smoke, talking about taking LSD. For some reason, the resulting story identified Jones as Jagger.

While this was going on, the Stones' new album, *Between the Buttons*, was released. It had different tracks in America, but the English album, though it had the odd great song, like 'Back Street Girl' and 'Connection,' was by far the lightest-weight long-playing effort the Stones had released, revealing perhaps the lack of road tensions, pleasure in the moment, enjoying being young and rich in one's hometown – all of which could lessen the dramatic content of one's productions. It sounded, one cruel but truthful listener said, 'like a Kinks album.' If the Stones were lost in complacency and a drug-induced euphoric haze, they were about to be sobered up.

The next Saturday, February 11, Keith, at the Courtfield Road flat with Brian and Anita, invited them and a big party of London aesthetes – including Mick and his *regulaire*, singer-actress Marianne Faithfull; photographer Michael Cooper; art dealer Robert Fraser and his Moroccan servant Mohamed; antique dealer Christopher Gibbs; Beatle George Harrison and his wife – to join him for the weekend at Redlands. As it turned out, when they were leaving Brian and Anita got into a fight. 'We just left them fighting,' Keith told me.

Sunday morning or early Sunday afternoon, Keith and some of his guests dropped acid, as the saying went. They went to the beach, wandered about the south coast, marveling at the wonders of God's universe, then by nightfall straggled back to the house. Keith took a bath; incense was

71

burning, a fire was on the hearth, and Mohamed was preparing dinner. George and Patti Harrison left, going back to London. Marianne, about to go upstairs for a bath, had taken off her clothes and was sitting by the fire, wrapped in a fur rug. If you had taken acid, you were tired but with a peaceful awareness, open, vulnerable. It was about eight o'clock when the police knocked. There were nineteen of them. 'I got busted before I was ready for it,' Keith said.

Nothing like it had ever happened to such a prominent group of entertainers. When the police left they took cannabis from Keith and amphetamines from Mick, and at the time any sort of illegal drug use on the part of youth idols was very probably career-destroying. Visions of Mick going back into theoretical economics, Keith working up a portfolio to show ad agencies, Brian . . . ah, Brian.

'At the Redlands '67 bust,' Keith said, 'the cops had been told to get it on with us. In my life, before 1967, the smorgasbord was grass or amphetamines. Smoking a bit of weed or taking some uppers. The amphetamines you get into as a musician right away because it's just to make the next gig, it goes with the job. Like the bomber pilot, if you've got to bomb Dresden tomorrow, everyone gets like four or five bennies to make the trip and keep themselves together. Well, you've got to drive five hundred miles right now and you got the gig in twelve hours, and these bands are bumpin' into each other – one guy says, "I can't make it" and another cat says, "Tell you how we make it. Have a few of these." Don't cost nothing anyway, you can get them anywhere. There was no legal interpretation on it to me; it didn't even occur to me. Twelve months later, the cops all got education, it's a crime. And if you been away most of that year, you still think it's just part of your life and your job, something you deal with yourself, nothing to do with anybody else.

'We got busted because of popularity, the drugs were just the excuse, the real issue was the effect we were thought to have on the rest of the population. I was no big acid freak, trying to push this stuff. "If you get a little too up there on them pills, smoke some of this . . ." That was my thing. But that's part of the industry. It always has been with musicians. They have their own ways of dealing with things and left to themselves it wouldn't be a big problem. What happened is that the audience got into the same bag and not for the same reasons. Musicians would be very happy if it was still – "Cool, man" – dressing-room shit, elitist.

'It became an issue. People started to write songs and sing about it and advocate it. And the rest of us are going, "Oh, man, unhip." You don't let that shit out of the dressing room. And suddenly it has become a major way of life in a matter of a few months. Then they want to look for somebody to blame, and we set ourselves up. "Would you let your daughter marry one?" We were easy meat. At least they thought we were.

'Brian really was an easy victim, but Brian was a suitable case for treatment. He needed to be in a fucking hospital. He needed help. But we were all working too hard to expect it from the guys you were working with. Then I get myself right out of the picture. I make friends again with Brian and then steal his old lady. So I really screwed up.'

After the police came to Redlands, host and guests scattered. Pausing only to confer with lawyers, Jagger, Faithfull, and Fraser flew to Morocco, while Richards, Pallenberg, and Jones went to France – Jones's chauffeur Tom Keylock driving 'The Blue Lena,' Richards's Bentley, named for Lena Horne. No matter what color the car became, it was still called that. Brian, true to form, took sick and went into a Toulon hospital. With an actress friend they'd picked up in Paris, Keith and Anita traveled on to Barcelona. In Barcelona, after getting into a fight with some (other) drunks and spending the night in jail, they were released in the morning to find Brian on the phone telling Anita to come back to Toulon. Heading for Africa, Richards and Pallenberg went to Valencia, where (or maybe in the car on the way there) they became lovers.

'Amazing things can happen in the back of a car,' Keith said, 'and they did. We split in the camouflage Bentley in the middle of the night and make a dash for Tangiers, arrived at the hotel, and found a stack of telegrams and messages from Brian, ordering Anita to go and pick him up.'

In a sort of compromise (not that there wasn't plenty of that involved already), Richards and Pallenberg drove to Marrakech, from whence, accompanied by Faithfull, Pallenberg flew to pick up Jones.

'We're all in Marrakech,' Keith said. 'Cecil Beaton's there, Robert Fraser, Brion Gysin, Mick, and the air's like heavy, lots of people doing acid. I'm feeling guilty.'

Brian, wandering around the city, in a tantrum of destructive behavior, procures an indigenous whore, brings her to the hotel, and tells Anita to get it on with her – at which juncture, God bless her brave good spirit, Anita said, in essence, 'Go shit in yer hat.' Big brouhaha ensues, to which stickiness Richards responds by having Brion Gysin take Jones away to hear some local musicians, giving Richards and Pallenberg the chance to depart. 'This is like the Sheik of Araby,' Keith said. Though it wasn't yet apparent to anybody except Anita, Keith had formed his style. When presented with a challenge, for many years to come, he would always do the heroic thing.

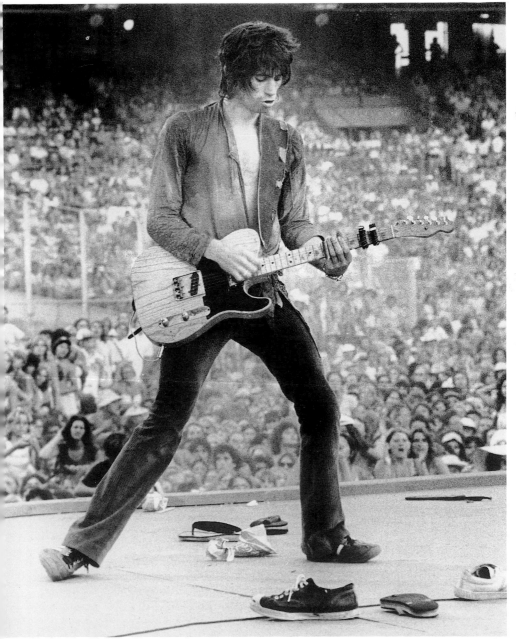

August 1978, Anaheim, California. Keith among shoes thrown by fans in tribute.

Keith wears leather, plays bass, 1975.

Madison Square Gardens, 1975, thinking about getting that tooth fixed,
'It's fallen out of favour with me.'

The Glimmer Twins, 1975, sweethearts together.

Cosmic cowboy, 1972.

Keith and Ronnie at Tracks nightclub in New York City celebrating the
release of *Love You Live*, September 1977.

Keith rides a riff, November, 1989.

Mick and Keith sing and play 'You Can't Always Get What You Want And Please Forgive Me.'

Keith, New York City, June 1978 on the *Some Girls* tour – Fender guitar, leather jacket, Moroccan scarf – the personification of World Boogie.

Ron Wood, Mick and Keith with Billy Preston looming just visible in the background, 1975. Keith would ultimately tire of session players on Stones tours – even good ones like Billy Preston.

Standing in the shadow, 1975.

against a metal cabinet. 'Aha!' he said, holding up a black guitar decorated with a painted sun-and-moon design. 'Look, it's green – the best guitar in England and it looks as if it's been in a flood.' He started cleaning it with a rag, then plugged it into an amplifier so the cleaning noises could be heard.

In one corner of the room stood a stainless steel coffee machine, complete with a set of blue-and-white-striped cups, a milk pitcher, and a box of sugar cubes. Keith put the guitar down, came and filled a cup. He spilled the milk, then overturned the sugar cubes onto the rug. He put the cubes back in the box, took two out again for his coffee, and went back to his stool beside Brian, who was taking an enormous bite of a meat pie. After two more bites Brian rewrapped the pie in waxed paper and put it on top of Keith's amplifier.

As Keith was tuning his guitar, his friends George and Spanish Tony came in. Spanish Tony (Sanchez; later to publish *Up and Down with the Rolling Stones*, and immortalized in Keith's lines, 'Scars healin' but the dealer's squealin' – the pool's in but the patio ain't dry,') has long black hair, lightly salted with gray, and is wearing yellow sunglasses. George, or perhaps Jorge, is also Spanish. He has long, long dark hair and dark eyes and is frequently seen casting hot looks from beneath his long dark lashes. Tuning a final string, Keith created feedback from his amplifier that became louder and louder until each separate vibration seemed to jar inside your head. When the noise stopped, he played two bass notes, a few chords, and a loping single-note pattern that summoned up echoes of Muddy Waters, Bo Diddley, and Jimmy Reed. The pattern, repeating, developed into a riff. Bill, holding his bass nearly upright, was touching the strings tentatively. Brian was using a bottleneck now, still reading *Melody Maker*. Charlie was swatting the drums with brushes, playing classic rhythm & blues patterns with the looseness of a jazz player, his face blank, eyes wide open. Spanish Tony

87

played the organ, which was unplugged and thus inaudible. George was dancing, shaking his mane, casting glances.

Finally Keith went into a long run of single notes, and the riff collapsed. The room was quiet. Brian removed a broken string from his guitar, took another from the guitar case, put it on the guitar, and turned another page. Charlie, using sticks now, hit the drums – whappa *whappa* whappa *whappa* – Keith played a phrase that perfectly fit the rhythm, Brian and Bill quickly picked up the chords, George started playing the congas, and Spanish Tony played wildly out-of-tune clanging note clusters on the piano. Keith grinned as the room began to vibrate from the sound.

CHAPTER 8

1968, continued:

This 'rehearsal' was no different from many the Stones have had during their years together, except that Mick the magic Jagger, as Andrew Oldham used to call him, the most public Stone, was on the other side of town, was becoming a movie star. Being already a Star, Mick required, it seemed, nothing more for this minor transfiguration than a little celluloid.

If he were, say, a university lecturer in economics, which from his background he might well have been (his father is a physical-education instructor at a Dartford teacher's college, his mother is a member of the local Conservative Association, and Mick himself was a scholarship student at the London School of Economics, of which U.S. President John F. Kennedy was an alumnus), he would be just an ugly young man with close-cropped hair and baggy three-button suits, thick lips and pop eyes. But he is not that; he is Mick Jagger, the only white rock performer worthy to be regarded, as a singer and dancer, alongside such black men as James Brown and Otis Redding. He is a strange, lithe, thin man whose hair, darkened for the movie, reaches his shoulders – in makeup, which he wore for most of his waking hours during the weeks when he was working on the film, he seemed part witch, part voluptuous boy. There are people who, by their presence, compel attention; Jagger is one of them.

The film was to be called *Performance*. According to the publicity handouts, it concerned, oddly enough, a pop star, 'a strange electronic poet, a latter-half-of-the-twentieth-century writer,' who, having retired from the pop scene with two young girls, the three of them planning to make beautiful music together, had the privacy of his opulent London house shattered by the unexpected arrival of a fugitive murderer, 'a suave professional criminal at odds both with his under-world colleagues and the police,' played by James Fox. 'But,' Mick said, 'it keeps changing every day.'

The film was being shot entirely on location in London. Except for a few exterior sequences, the filming was done in two houses – one in Hyde Park Gate, down the street from the house where Winston Churchill died, and one in Chelsea, on fashionable tree-shaded Lowndes Square. Mick arrived at one place or the other at eight o'clock in the morning and left at seven at night, six days a week. When he was not on the set, he spent a lot of time talking to reporters, most of whom asked the same questions.

One day a young man from *Photoplay* wearing a glen plaid suit, orange shirt, and red paisley tie went into the room (Mick called it 'our only haven of insanity') where the actors relaxed, or tried to, between takes. Two minutes later he was out again. 'I asked him why he went into films, and he shrugged. I asked whether the part he's playing resembled the real-life Jagger, and he said, "No!" (Mick had given the opposite answer to other interviewers.) 'I asked if he were enjoying making the film, and he said, "Sometimes." When I asked if he'd enlarge on that, he refused. Then I said, "You're really quite difficult, aren't you?" To that he said, "Yes." '

The next interviewer, a newspaper reporter, was inundated by Eau de Lanvin. But still they came, and left, saying, 'I thought he was supposed to be an intelligent bloke. What's the matter with him?'

'I don't envy you your work, writing about the Stones,' a Warner Brothers publicity writer told me, one afternoon at the house on Lowndes Square. He was from Philadelphia, but he had been around. You could see that. He was wearing a dark blue dress shirt, his quietly checked suit fit him, his shoes had buckles, and he had one of those expensive haircuts that look like a skullcap with sideburns. 'This Jagger – I don't know, maybe he's a good singer, if you like that kind of music, but as a person—' He curled his lip. 'We've had a few words. At lunch one day I said to him – Know what I said? I said, "Are you just naturally rude, or did you have to study?" Hrr hrr. "Did you have to study?" Hrr hrr. Listen, is there any information I can give you?'

'What's that you're sitting on?' He was riding sidesaddle on a three-sided partition, built out from the wall. 'This? This is the shower. Really works,' he said, pointing up to the dripping nozzle. The partition was covered with what looked like blue-and-white porcelain tile but was actually, the publicity man told me, painted fiberglass. 'There's a scene where Jagger and the girls take a shower. Set'll probably be closed for that. Hrr.'

I nodded, looking around the big, crowded room. You could not take a full step in any direction without running into something, and there were a bewildering number of things to run into: cameras on tripods, great banks of lights, boom mikes on silvery branches, writhing cables, lethargic technicians and prop men, all arranged in a kind of semicircle around a narrow bed, a marble fireplace, and a low table. The Moroccan bed was almost indescribably ornate, like thousands of tiny colored spools stuck together; the fireplace, wide but shallow, had two large brass andirons shaped like lions on pedestals; the mosaic table held a pair of heavy gold candlesticks, a pink conch shell, and a package of Rizla cigarette papers. The dark red wall was partly hung with

93

tapestries, and the floor was covered with cushions and Persian rugs. On the far side of the bed rested an antique rocking horse.

Sitting on the bed were the two directors of the film: Donald Cammell, a young man with longish brown hair, and Nicholas Roeg, a heavyset man with a bald spot. Cammell had written the screenplay for a film called *Duffy*, Roeg had been a cameraman on many films, among them *The Trials of Oscar Wilde*, *The Sundowners*, *A Funny Thing Happened on the Way to the Forum*, *Fahrenheit 451*, and *Petulia*, but this was each man's debut as a director.

Cammell stood up, wiping his hands on the seat of his pants, and yelled 'Props!' A boy brought in a couple of bottles of Alsatian white wine and a large bowl of salad. A prop man doused the logs in the fireplace with something called Whiz and ignited them with a cigarette lighter. They burst briefly into flame and then began to smolder, filling the room with smoke. Some of the lights came on and shone through the sinuous blue wisps. Mick came in and started coughing. He was wearing white linen trousers, a white shirt with ruffled front and flared cuffs, and black-and-gold slippers. Around his neck was a flexible gold necklace shaped like a snake. Cammell took the snake's head in his fingers. 'Bit of a problem with the smoke, love,' he said.

'I'll wait upstairs,' Mick said, still coughing.

'We'll call you.'

As Mick left the room, he passed his costar, James Fox, who came in wearing a blue suit with bloodstains. His right eye was decorated with a purplish yellow bruise. He saw the smoke, said something under his breath, and went out.

'Can we open a window?' Roeg asked.

'They won't open,' Cammell said. 'I'm trying to get a fan.'

A prop man had left two brown paper bags on the table. Roeg opened one, finding it full of plump white mushrooms. 'Are these fresh? Are they edible?' Roeg and Cammell sat down and began eating. Wineglasses, silver, and three china plates were brought in. A tall brunette girl in a red dress came into the room and stretched out on the bed. 'She's the director's assistant,' the publicity man told me. Around them the lights were going up, down, off, back up again. It was getting hard to see across the room through the smoke. The young man with the Whiz came and stood by the fireplace. 'That's not the right sort of draft system,' he said.

'Maybe we'd better not see the fire in the shot,' said Cammell, serving the plates with salad. The prop man left the room, followed after a moment by Roeg. Then the girl left. Cammell stood up, found himself alone, and went out.

A moment later they were all back again, with more prop men and technicians, and a large red tank marked CALORPROPANE.

'What do we do next?' Cammell asked.

Roeg sat on the bed, looking morosely at the table. 'Salad dressing?'

A gray-haired technician in a tweed suit was fixing a rubber hose to the top of the red tank. Two prop men were standing before the fireplace. 'Won't burn at all,' one said.

'It will either burn or it won't,' Cammell said. 'This sort of thing should be tested.'

'Mick had it burning beautifully the other day,' the girl said. 'Maybe we should ask him to start it.'

The technician put on overalls over his tweeds and, with the help of the young man who had Whizzed in the fireplace, carried the red tank within range of the smoking logs. Kneeling, he aimed the rubber hose and pressed a trigger. Gas roared out as from a dragon's nostril, searing the logs. They began to crackle and burn. 'Well,' Cammell said. 'We might as well start shooting.'

'Could we have a rehearsal?' Roeg called to the room at large. Mick came in with James Fox, who spoke briefly to Cammell and went back out. Cammell lay down beside the fireplace on a mound of cushions, showing Mick how he should be placed. Anita Pallenberg, the blonde actress from

Italy who used to be Brian's girlfriend, is now Keith's, and who is playing Mick's, came in and sat by the table. Mick took off his slippers and white socks. His toenails were painted bright red. 'Whoo,' said the publicity man. A lighting man was bounding around the room taking readings with a handheld meter. The candles on the table were lighted. Mick stretched out on the cushions, yawning. 'Just a few minutes, love,' Cammell told him.

Fox came back in, wearing a false mustache, a double-breasted blue chalkstripe suit, a gray felt hat, and an old-fashioned red necktie. 'That suits you,' Mick said. Fox sat on the bed and, looking into a compact mirror, applied a lipcut from a small makeup bottle. Cammell gave him a plate of salad and passed a goblet of wine to Mick, who started immediately to drink. The smoke in the room was slowly clearing.

'Could we rehearse it?' Cammell asked.

'Yes, *please*,' Roeg said.

In the scene they were about to do, the publicity man told me, James Fox, wanting a disguised photograph so that he can get a passport and leave the country, pretends to be a juggler looking for a new image and asks Miss Pallenberg to take some pictures of him with Mick's Polaroid camera. The scene, which lasts only a few seconds, begins with Miss Pallenberg peeling a photograph off the developing plate and giving it to Fox, who looks at it and says, 'I never wear hats, not normally.'

'Not when you're performing?' Mick asks.

'No,' Fox says. 'I never wear hats.' Miss Pallenberg asks him how he likes the salad, and Fox, a gentleman despite his appearance, says that she is a good cook.

Before this bit of action could take place, a photograph of Fox was needed. The assembled company waited through one sixty-second Polaroid excitement after another until a usable picture came along. Miss Pallenberg was placed so that a camera could look over her shoulder. Then Roeg said, 'All right. Full rehearsal.'

'From the top, please,' Cammell said.

'Where's the photograph?' Miss Pallenberg asked. They found it, after a while, on the table, and the rehearsal started. But it stopped almost immediately because Miss Pallenberg, giving the picture to Fox, raised herself out of camera range. On the next attempt, Cammell halted the action to adjust Fox's hat, which had sunk past his eyebrows. There were, in all, twelve trials before Cammell said, 'Hold it. Let's try it once more with the cameras on.' None of the interruptions was caused by Mick, whose face became more like a mask with each one.

Once more props, positions, camera angles were checked. Makeup men and girls came back, retouched Fox's wounds, dusted Miss Pallenberg's brow, and powdered Mick's cheeks and nose. The red tank of CALOR was brought in again to punch up the fire, which had been burning brightly for some time. The technician squatted before the fireplace, nodded to Mick, who was lying directly beside it, squeezed the trigger, and produced a rush of gas that caused the hearth to erupt in a whirlwind of snow-white ashes. Mick, enveloped in them, leaped to his feet, laughing devilishly. 'Is this how we want it?' he said, dancing through the floating flakes. 'Can we film it now?'

Finally, after the ashes had settled, with the cameras in place, the actors properly painted and positioned, the company was ready at last to film the scene – except that it was, somebody noticed, seven o'clock, Official Union Closing Time. 'We'll get an early start tomorrow, Mick,' Cammell promised, but Mick was already out the door.

One pleasant evening, a few minutes after seven o'clock, I came out of the house in Lowndes Square where *Performance* was being filmed, and there was Keith in the Bentley.

'Waiting for Mick?' I asked, all ignorance.

'Waitin' for Anita.' I didn't know about all the intrigue,

didn't know about Brian and Anita, didn't know how little trust existed in sleepy London town.

In Victor Bockris's book about Keith, he quotes Ian Stewart: 'Keith refused to go into the Lowndes Square house and often parked outside and sent messages in to Anita. As for Anita and Mick, I always felt there was no love lost there; they always seemed to be a bit wary of each other, but when the big sex scene of the movie was filmed, instead of simulating sex they really got into each other, and although what wound up in the picture was a lot of vague, tumbling bodies in the sheets, nothing explicit, there was a lot of very explicit footage of Mick and Anita really screwing, steamy, lusty stuff, that was edited into a separate X-rated short feature that was shown all around and actually copped an award at some X-rated film festival in Amsterdam.

'Of course, Keith got hold of this and was pissed at what he saw. For a while things were strained between him and Mick, and of course things were pretty rough with Anita.'

So here I am, completely oblivious to anything not in my own fat head, telling Keith, who's sitting outside this house where his woman and his best friend are betraying him, as he and his woman had betrayed her previous man – instant-karma fashion, though Lennon hadn't written the phrase yet – about this idea I had. It was a magazine cover for the story I was writing. At the time, the news magazines were full of rock 'n' roll and war. (*Time*'s cover story dated April 15, 1966, proclaimed 'London the Swinging City,' and shared space with news of the increasing intensity of U.S. bombing attacks on North Vietnam.) My tasteful scheme was to procure a helicopter from a nearby U.S. Air Force base and photograph the Rolling Stones in American uniforms with severed Vietnamese heads. Charlie would be the pilot in olive-drab tank top, mirror aviator shades, and bill cap; Bill Wyman, in a vest hung with grenades, would stand in the chopper's cargo door; and Mick, Keith, and Brian, armed with various weaponry, were to pose behind a line of dark-haired decapitees.

I figured the photo would with any luck at all provoke outrage in the U.S. of A.

'Get it together and we'll do it,' Keith said.

The cover never happened, but not because Keith wasn't willing. My point in telling this story is not political – just that Keith didn't take a long time making decisions. 'Politics,' he has said, 'are what we were trying to get away from in the first place.'

One night the Stones met Jean-Luc Godard at the Stones' office. *One Plus One* was having its premiere showing at the London Film Festival, and the Stones were to be photographed with Godard for one of the London newspapers.

The building which houses the office is in the London downtown business district, on the corner of Maddox and St. George streets, conveniently close to St. George's Church. Listed on the office registry at the entrance, along with the World Model Agency: Fastback Productions, Associated American Newspapers, Ltd., and Brocklehurst Fabrics, there is the Rolling Stones, Ltd. One walks up eight steep flights or rides the lift with not more than three other people, whom he will have the leisure and proximity to get to know very well before the car reaches its stop.

The lift is old, the building is old, the office is old – the floorboards creak – but the walls of the place have been freshly painted white, and the furniture, though secondhand, has been refurbished. It is a place where a good amount of hard work is done by five people (the Stones' employees, not the Stones) but the atmosphere is homelike and comfortable. In the main room – where Georgia Bergman, the mistress of the office, standing at not quite five feet, usually sits, talking into two telephones at once – there are a small blue couch, a Singer sewing machine, an antique desk, a round white table, and two steamer trunks, one of which bears the name of S. E. W. Waller, Royal Fusiliers. On the wall there is a Pear's Soap advertisement showing a little black baby being washed white; on the table, a copy of *Women's Work*, the magazine of the Methodist Missionary Society; on one of the trunks, what may be the last remaining copy of *Love Among the Ruins*, by Warwick Deeping; and on the door to the rest room there is a sign saying LADIES.

Charlie arrived first, followed shortly by Brian. They were sitting in the main room talking about Brian's Moroccan album when Godard came in, a small, intense man wearing dark glasses and a trench coat. While the Coasters sang 'Save the Last Dance for Me,' Charlie and Brian chatted with the director. 'Are you working now, or resting?' Charlie asked.

'At the moment, you mean?' asked Godard, who speaks English uncertainly.

'He means, are you making a film now,' Brian explained.

'Oh.' Godard shrugged modestly. 'Two or three.'

Getting the Stones together is not easy. 'I can never quite believe it when all of them actually show up,' Miss Bergman said, but soon Mick came in, and then Bill and Keith (who even then was demonstrating that until he arrived, the party hadn't started), and the photographer had been kept waiting only an hour. A nervous man with a beard, he herded the group into the back room, where he had set up his lights and tripod. The back room, the conference room of the Stones' office, resembles the dining room of an old-fashioned cottage, with a large oval table on which there was a bowl of grapes and oranges, a wooden hutch that held glass jars of raisins, pumpkin and sunflower seeds, and vases of fresh red and white carnations and sweetheart roses. The photographer arranged the Stones around M. Godard on an L-shaped couch.

For the next hour, he pushed them together, pulled them apart, arranging and rearranging as the lights glared and the shutter snapped. He referred to Brian as 'that one' – 'Could you ask that one to look at the camera?' The Stones paid less and less attention to his requests, until the photographer was forced to call them to order. 'All right, now,' he said. 'Look menacing.' They dissolved in laughter, and he turned his attention to the genius of the *nouvelle vague*, who was directed to sit, stand, lean this way and that. M. Godard seemed to become smaller, darker, and more intense with each command, until the photographer, taking a chair from the table, placed it in reversed position before the couch. 'Sit here,' he said. 'Like this,' showing M. Godard how to straddle the chair.

'No,' said the revolutionary *cinéasle*.

'All right,' said the photographer. 'What do you want to do?'

M. Godard looked thoughtful, then turned the chair around and sat in it.

Still trying valiantly, the photographer began to pose the Stones around Godard. 'All in close now, please – could you get a little higher?'

'We can get a lot higher than this,' Mick told him, as the Stones collapsed laughing, and that was the end of the photo session.

I had, during those autumnal weeks in London, memorable strolls, getting stranded by the Thames after walking with Georgia Bergman, the Stones' secretary, and actor Howard Hesseman past the Houses of Parliament, wandering in Hyde Park, beside the Serpentine, where Peter Pan landed, with Sir Brian: For some reason, Brian relaxes me; he's, if anything, crazier than I am, and strange as it may seem I feel perfectly safe with him. At the moment I'm berating him and, by extension, his bandmates – 'I know people talk about the Beatles, that four-headed monster, but you guys, you're at the opposite extreme, you don't even know each other.'

Brian giggles tragically in the slanting sunshine. 'No,

really, it's not true – I ring Mick, Mick and Keith and I ring each other, we talk—' Poor angel baby, brokenhearted spirit. Requiescat in pace, *pauvre ange*.

The *Eye* article appeared in March and April of 1969. It was an unsettled time, the first half of that year, and I wrote about things as they came along, a great new band called the Flying Burrito Brothers, a piece about the Memphis Blues Festival. On July 3 at about four in the morning I lay in bed and listened as the phone rang twelve times. Then I answered: Georgia Bergman was calling to tell me that Brian had been found dead in his swimming pool. Less than a month before, Keith, Mick and Charlie had asked Brian to leave the Rolling Stones. Anita was pregnant with Keith's baby. Brian saw his whole life going wrong. He's had babies, more than enough, but Anita was his destiny, now forever lost.

'Mick and I went to see Brian,' Keith said, 'and say, "Look, this is not going to work. You're pulling all these strokes, why don't we just make this thing sane? We're gettin' *Let It Bleed* together, and you ain't there, and you're not really in the band. You got a nice house here, I think you're better off following your own nose."

'What we were trying to say was a very difficult thing. After all, Brian was the guy that kicked Stu out of the band. In a way it's like the script starts to take shape after this. And the guy that kicked Stu out of the band is the first one to croak.'

The Stones were at Olympic, recording 'I Don't Know Why,' a Stevie Wonder song, when the news came. Jock, the old Scottish attendant there, told me that Keith took the news particularly hard.

On July 5, Decca released the Stones' recording of Keith's modern Jimmie Rodgers song, 'Honky Tonk Woman,' and its flip side, a truncated 'You Can't Always Get What You Want.' I asked Stu who played guitar on 'Honky Tonk Woman,' and he said, 'Keith. About five times, with all the overdubs.' It would become the Stones' third number-one single in the United States. Only the third. The Stones have never been as popular as whatever current sensation was happening – Debbie Boone, Michael Jackson, or Whitney Houston – but they have proved the truth of Oldham's contention: They are a way of life.

That same day in Hyde Park, the Stones, with their new guitar player, young blond Mick Taylor, played a free concert attended by at least a quarter of a million people, the Stones' biggest audience so far. Already shaken by the necessity of firing Brian, Keith and Mick had wanted to make a major splash with the new single and album. Then I heard that the Stones planned to tour the U.S. in the fall, for the first time in three years, since their drug arrests. I decided that it might be worth doing a book about the Rolling Stones, who were so funky that one of them was a dead man. It wasn't only older celebrity figures like Dr. Martin Luther King, Jr. and the Kennedys or people embroiled in that unfortunate war who were dying, it was us. Interesting.

CHAPTER 9

How can people think that artists seek a name? A name, like a face, is something you have when you're not alone.

Annie Dillard, *Holy the Firm*

On August 10 in London, Marlon Richards was born. As soon as possible, Keith and Anita went to Redlands. Hanging out with Anita and the baby, Keith caved in, had to admit he was content: Wild horses, he thought, couldn't drag me away. 'You got my heart, you got my soul,' he sang to Anita. That's how it was.

'Keith changed,' Anita said. 'He had to give up that boyish, tough-guy act. The Stones could never have kept going if he hadn't.'

On October 17, the Stones flew to Los Angeles to mix their new album, *Let It Bleed*, and rehearse for their upcoming tour. On October 19, I joined them. Georgia Bergman and Howard Hessemann were good enough to pick me up at LAX, and we drove past the oil wells and billboards across Sunset and up Doheny where I'd seen Hoagie Carmichael crossing the street to a house rented from the Du Ponts, 1401 Oriole Drive, high above Sunset Strip. Charlie and Shirley Watts were there, along with Bill Wyman, who was even then the Grand Old Man of Teenybopperoni, and his Swedish Ice Princess, Astrid. Mick and Keith had left their women at home.

We sat listening to Count Basie's Kansas City rhythm

section playing with Lester Young and Buck Clayton and discussed various matters of life and death. In a few minutes Keith and Mick came in with Mick Taylor, producers Glyn Johns and Jimmy Miller, and Gram Parsons.

The previous fall in London, one of the most-played records in the Stones' office had been the Byrds' album, *Sweetheart of the Rodeo*, featuring Gram, who as a new member had apparently mesmerized the folk-rockers, converting them to Christian Cowboys. They'd come through London, where Gram had met Keith, on the way to play South Africa – but Keith told Gram the audiences there were segregated, nobody plays there – and Gram left the band. Earlier this year he released the first album, *Gilded Palace of Sin*, by his new band, the Flying Burrito Brothers. I had reviewed it for *Rolling Stone*.

Gram was from my hometown, Waycross, Georgia, though we'd never met, both having left young for different destinations. Now the force of something, call it the boogie disease, had washed us up on the other side of the country. Through Keith we became friends.

'My only problem with Gram,' Keith said, years after Gram's death, 'was Mick, because that was the first time I noticed that there was some weird thing that anybody that was a friend of mine, it didn't matter whether he wanted to be their friend – "You can't have him." A very, very possessive thing. Not that Mick and I ever hung out that much. We had different tastes. One of the ways we've been able to work together for so long is that we have always been able to accept that fact, that we have different tastes in the way we want to live. That was the first time I noticed that there was some tension between Mick and me because somebody else had gotten close to me. It may have happened before but I never noticed it. Mick had met a bigger gentleman. The biggest gent that I have ever known. Gram got the picture right away. We used to talk about it – "Are you and I going to be friends, or are we going to let somebody else dictate

108

whether we can know each other?" And Gram would say, "But for you it's important. This cat, you work with him, you know—" He saw it all straight away.

'The thing about Mick and me is that we never had to be that close, we never have been – we've just known each other a long time. The more we know each other, the more difficult it gets, in a way. This is chemistry we're talkin'. But for some reason Mick has a hard-on – he'll get incredibly shitty against anybody who appears to be getting too close to me. I don't know what it is. I just wish that he found a few guys that he got along with. Some of my friends are the biggest bums in the world, but they have some saving grace somewhere, and if other guys don't see it, well, that's cool. But don't get 'em beaten up, just because you don't see it. It's all right for one friend not to get along with another – it's another thing for somebody to try and do something about it. A friend to me is one of the blessings, more and more, as I go along. And I don't go along with this thing about, "You can count your best friends on one hand—" If that's so, you ain't farmin' the right acres. Because friends are everywhere.'

Maybe so, but as it happened, we ended up, that first night together, October 19, 1969, at the Yamato-E, a trendy late-sixties L.A. Japanese restaurant, where the atmosphere wasn't entirely friendly. As we were preparing to leave, a (grown-up) man and woman encountered Keith coming back from the toilet. 'You'd be cute,' the woman said, 'if you put a rinse on your hair.'

'You'd be cute,' Keith told her, 'if you put a rinse on your cunt.'

That night we went to the Ash Grove, a folk club in L.A., and heard Taj Mahal's band and the blues originator Arthur Crudup. Standing with Keith and Stu and the Stones hearing 'That's All Right, Mama' – the first Elvis Presley release – performed by its author with Taj's band rocking behind him, was to be poised for a precious few moments between the future and the past of the world's most vital music, perhaps the world's strongest cultural force.

◨

The country was different from the one the Stones had come to for the first time in 1964. The Rolling Stones were different, too; even the ones left alive were changed. They had been young before – no, they were still young, mid-twenties, except for Wyman – they had been adolescent before, still growing. Now they were playing to an audience of their peers, not simply hordes of shrilling teenyboppers. Now there were Vietnam vets at Stones shows. America and the Stones had worked profound changes in each other, and now they were getting together again – with many differences. Boys with crew cuts five years before now had waist-length tresses. For the first time, the Stones could hear themselves instead of a wall of pubescent shrieking. For the first time, the Stones played every night to stoned audiences. There was (nevertheless) a genuine feeling of communion. 'The myth that was widely believed,' Keith said, 'was that it was something more than entertainment.' Keith and the Stones certainly tried to make it that.

With a symmetry to rival Greek or any other kind of tragedy, the play unfolded, the Stones bringing the greatest music of their lives to the United States. Keith spent hours each day, when there were hours to spend, talking trans-atlantic baby talk to Marlon and Anita. The first heroic effort he had to accomplish on that tour was the pulling together of a set composed only of the songs the new kid could play. Luckily, the new kid was Mick Taylor. He seemed younger than springtime then, because Keith at twenty-six looked – as Michael Lydon, who covered that tour for the *New York Times*, observed – like Isak Dinesen, who had died seven years before of advanced syphilis. But Mick Taylor wasn't as young as he seemed; he was twenty-one, or two years older than the Stones when they started out. He'd had a thorough grounding with John Mayall's Bluesbreakers.

Another necessary task was to release the new album. It may be that you have to have human sacrifices to make an album as good as that one. Releasing the album involved rejecting the first pressing, which had been limited – a sound-engineering process that was the norm in America and may still be, wherein the highest and lowest frequencies get suppressed. 'Makes all the difference to a record,' Keith said. They sent it back to be unlimited. Mixing the album had for Keith involved riding herd on his tracks. While Mick and engineer Glyn Johns oversaw the bigger picture, Keith, sitting in a cloud of marijuana and tobacco smoke at the console, punched up the sound of his guitar just where, when, and for how long he wanted it.

The Stones rehearsed at the soundstage on the Warner brothers' film lot where the movie *They Shoot Horses, Don't They?* was shot, a marathon-dance ballroom, perfect setting. The music business had changed a great deal since the last time they toured the U.S., in 1966. Serious musicians like Crosby, Stills, Nash, and Young had appeared on the rock scene, guys who played tastefully and in tune. Such players carried their own sound systems and prided themselves on the quality of acoustic experience they could provide audiences. For the Stones tour, Ampeg lent the Stones a great many amplifiers, and the Stones plugged them in. Mick Taylor was appalled at the noise. Stu told him that if he didn't play as loud as Keith, he might as well play rhythm.

There were groupies and diversions about, but not for Keith; every night after rehearsals he, Gram and I sat around listening to blues and gospel records. There was a great purity, a genuine dedication, about the Stones' – and Gram's – pursuit of music. It was not for personal gain or glory; at least it didn't seem to be, not even for Mick, at least not then. Mick was jealous of Gram, that was obvious. He would be rude to Gram in petty ways, and Gram would treat him with amusement, like a man dealing with a teething puppy. What was it for – what were they pursuing? It would be unfair not to say wisdom, and perhaps not overstating the case to say God. Keith and Gram delighted in turning each other on, as we said then, to things they hadn't heard: Gram was the master at that, bringing Dorothy Norwood and Dorothy Love Coates, (Spector's favorite singer) and Magic Sam and Lonnie Mack and many George Jones, Merle Haggard, Hank Williams, and Porter Wagoner songs to our attention. We lived to unearth lines like Washington Phillips's '. . . you can go to college, you can go to school, but if you ain't got Jesus, you's a educated fool.' Long-haired dopers in sissy outfits we may have been, but scratch one of us and you find a disciple, a missionary, a Jesuit.

What shaped the Stones' 1969 tour was a delicate system of influences. Greeting them on their arrival in America was a column from the San Francisco jazz critic Ralph Gleason saying that their ticket prices were outrageous and that they despised their audience. Gleason was one of the founding fathers of the magazine *Rolling Stone*, and being criticized by him carried some weight even with the Stones. They didn't think he accused them justly, and they were willing to demonstrate their unity with the people and the social changes taking place. This would very nearly prove their undoing.

At the end of 1969, the U.S.A. was at war in Vietnam; the peace of American cities was a banked fire ready to erupt with any spark into a conflagration. Merle Haggard's 'Okie from Muskogee' was on the pop charts. The Woodstock Festival had taken place the previous August. All things for good or evil seemed possible. The Stones' shows with Brian had contained patches of brilliance like the guitar solo on 'I Wanna Be Your Man' and the marimba on 'Under My Thumb,' but the best Stones' shows I ever heard were the ones with Mick Taylor. In time the mixture grew confining, even to Keith, but in the beginning, when they were putting together a set out of what Stones songs the new kid could play, it was exhilarating.

The tour opened out of town at the Colorado State University Fort Collins campus, then premiered at the Forum in Los Angeles. The Memphis blues singer Booker White, in town to play a gig with the Burritos at a folk club, came by the Forum with Gram. Seeing Keith's National, the same guitar Booker played, he asked Keith to play a bit. Listening, Booker held a hand over Keith's head and proclaimed to the dressing room, 'This a star, here. This a Hollywood star. If I'm lyin', I'm dyin'.' It was the sweetest moment – Keith started playing 'Key to the Highway,' Mick started singing, both of them performing for Booker, a scene of kindness and mutual respect, very lovely.

Before the 1969 tour the Stones' concerts had been brief incandescences, like Roman candles. Mick had worn high-heeled boots, the better for stomping. In Los Angeles in the fall of 1969 he bought beaded Indian moccasins, real ones, for dancing on the purple starburst carpet the Stones toured with that year. The 1969 shows were Art, with Mick portraying a figure that varied between manic sexiness ('a rooster on acid,' a comedian called him), violence, and in the acoustics blues numbers he and Keith did, a remarkably un-self-conscious reverence. The reverence for the music had to do with the wisdom of the traditional songs they sang, like 'You Got To Move,' with its recurring acceptance:

You may be high, you may be low
You may be rich, child, you may be po'
But when the Lord gets ready, you got to move.

The Stones played Oakland, San Diego . . . every night there was tension between the cops – whom the Stones had tried to ban from the arenas, insisting on no uniforms – and the

113

crowds, sweet-tempered stoned young folk just wantin' to boogie. In Oakland Keith asked me to go out and get him – actually he had Sam Cutler, author of the phrase 'the greatest rock 'n' roll band in the world, the Rolling Stones,' ask me to go out and bring back – a bottle of bourbon, brand name 'Old Charlie'. Took me a while in a by-no-means-friendly-to-white-boys neighborhood on a Sunday evenin' to decipher the cockney culture shock and come up with Old Charter. Mick wanted me to write out their song lists, too. They knew that, except for themselves and Stu, I was the tour's only pro. Phoenix; Dallas; Auburn, Alabama; touring the U.S. with Ike and Tina Turner, B.B. King, and Chuck Berry. Night after night there was the feeling that if all of this happened outside the reach of authority it might really make a difference. So much youth and beauty, why not have another festival to say good night to the sixties? Why not? By the time the Stones reached New York they'd decided to do something of the sort, some species of free concert, at the end of the tour.

The Stones played Detroit, Philadelphia, Boston, Madison Square Garden, then flew to Florida to play the West Palm Beach Pop Festival, a cold, wet, embattled thing. That completed the tour, and they went to Muscle Shoals to cut some tracks. The plane the Stones were offered by the transportation manager for the tour, who had told Chrysler he was working for the Stones and the Stones he was working for Chrysler, was so ugly that Mick and I wouldn't get on it. Wyman didn't either, but Keith, Charlie, and little Mick did, so they arrived at Muscle Shoals a day ahead of us.

There, at Muscle Shoals Sound Studio, the Stones cut 'You Got to Move,' 'Brown Sugar,' and 'Wild Horses.' The last, a love song Keith had written for Anita, was changed by Mick, who'd been abandoned by Marianne. While Mick's touring America, Marianne ran off from London to Italy with a film director. Keith had hundreds of songs in those days, and when the Stones needed one, he'd go off in a room by himself for a few minutes and come back with one. This time Mick went off and came back with new lyrics except for the chorus, adding a bittersweet quality to the tenderness. Keith thought, and said, it was beautiful.

Makes you wonder how it comes to occur on pages 179 and 180 of Victor Bockris's Keith book that 'Gram Parsons made major contributions to "Wild Horses," ' and 'Jagger was . . . particularly jealous of Keith's relationship with Gram as they began to work on "Wild Horses" together.'

Gram was my friend, and I'm always delighted to credit his great talent. But he didn't have any direct influence on 'Wild Horses' whatever. Later, after the Stones cut it – they were playing it that night at the Huntington after Altamont; Gram heard it then – Gram asked if the Burritos could cut it, and they did. 'The first time I heard it was after Altamont,' Gram said. 'We were all just shaking with the whole experience. They were leaving the next day. And they said, "I want you to hear these songs," and they played "Wild Horses" and "Brown Sugar." They'd recorded them in Muscle Shoals about a week or two before. [Not so long, actually.] I asked Mick if we could put it on our next album if we didn't release it as a single, and he said all right.' Bockris is equally questionable when he claims that Charlie Watts is 'occasionally a heavy drinker' and Bobby Keys a racist. I've known Charlie since 1968 and observed him in many situations including as a guest in his house. I have never known Charlie to drink to excess. Bobby, whom I have known since 1972, is one of the greatest admirers of traditional ethnic musicians.

The Stones stayed in Muscle Shoals, eating the canned soup at the Holiday Inn, for three nights while recording, then flew to San Francisco, where the free concert was to be held.

Altamont came about for many reasons, among them the Isle of Wight, Woodstock, Hyde Park. The time called for festivals, so festivals took place. There seemed a dawning awareness that wherever three or four hundred thousand were gathered together in the name of three-chord blues and illegal sacraments, the letter of the law signified naught. At any rate, no matter what anybody says, the Rolling Stones didn't hire the Hell's Angels as security, whether for beer, love, or money. The festival was free; you couldn't keep anybody out. The Angels came and behaved like Angels among the hundreds of thousands of hippies, and people died. One, an eighteen-year-old black man named Meredith Hunter, pulled a gun in front of the stage and was killed by Angels. The film *Gimme Shelter* gives the impression that Hunter was killed and everyone immediately left. From the amount of violence I'd seen – people hit over the head with weighted pool cues and so on – I assumed the Angels had killed many people, but you couldn't know for sure if you were onstage, where the Stones remained for another hour, giving one of the best performances of their lives, facing chaos and old night.

The myth persists that the Stones hired the Hell's Angels to serve as security guards at Altamont. 'We just walked into a situation,' Keith said. 'It happened to be 1969 in America. We left it all to the Grateful Dead. It's not a blame thing. We just said, "You cats do these free concerts all the time, how do you do it?" We were at the end of a long tour and we were recording in Muscle Shoals. We said, "Yes, we do want to try and do this free concert in San Francisco." Because that was the spirit of the times. There seemed to be a need to do it. It was just a thank you. We got to go to Frisco to do this free concert and we don't even know where the hell it's going to be. They keep shifting the location. It's become a big deal, now we're in there and we can't get out. There is no blame attached to anybody including the Angels, it's just there you saw chaos without anarchy. There was no hope of anarchy. In retrospect, it might have been far worse. Once you got one stiff on the ground – that's amazing that it stopped there.'

Reminded that he was the only person onstage who had the bright idea to point to individual Angels, yelling, 'Make that one stop!' when they were in their dream of omnipotence, Keith said, 'I don't think I could keep my mouth shut in a situation like that. What Mick was saying wasn't having much effect, Mick pleading for brotherhood. So I just pretended that there was somebody there to say, "Stop that mother fucker." Because if there's nobody else willing – There were five hundred thousand people out there. They could stop them anytime they want. There was what, how many of them, sixty, I thought there was Ripple and bad acid. The guy that got knocked off, in a way he asked for it. I asked for it, too, by opening my goddamn trap.

'I've always had the dirty job. My whole life. I don't know why, but when something's so obvious to you, thoughts go out the window – you just react: "You just threw me that ball, baby, now let me see what I can do with it. You posed the question." And actually – the Hell's Angels – I don't give a shit about a few guys who ride Harley-Davidsons. Why should I? I'm a guitar player. I jeopardized everybody there at Altamont with that thing, but it was something to me that just had to be said or all control was gonna be lost. Mick was sort of begging, "Please, please." I'd seen the way things were goin', the cops had disappeared, they don't wanta know, there's too many people and they just weren't prepared for this shit. Out there. Then.'

The action at Altamont could make a really interesting modern ballet. Arriving in the middle of the evening in San Francisco Keith, Mick, and I drove from the Huntington Hotel out to this automobile raceway near Livermore, the Altamont Speedway. We were going in a helicopter but the copter couldn't be found. So in the dead vast and middle of the night we found ourselves with an out-of-gas limo among campfires on a windy California hillside, drinking from great red jugs of wine offered by early arrivers. After viewing the desolation of this dark barren ground, Mick and I went back to the hotel to get some sleep, but Keith, Mr. Adventure, stayed at the site in a little trailer that would be backstage as soon as they got the stage finished.

In the morning Mick and I returned, with little Mick and Charlie. Wyman couldn't get it together to leave with us, and his failure to do so – not any desire of the Stones to go on late, so as to have moonlit human sacrifice – caused the Stones' appearance at the festival to be delayed until after dark.

Just as the helicopter landed and we got out, a crazed boy ran up and hit Mick in the mouth, completely uncalled-for, bizarre behavior. Enough to make a man question the wisdom of coming there. But we made it through the by-then enormous crowd to the trailer, where we sat with Keith and Gram, smoking grass, singing country songs and waiting for Wyman. We heard reports of violent incidents involving Hell's Angels, but we couldn't see what was happening, the crowd was too thick to venture among, and we kept waiting.

When at last Wyman arrived, the Stones went out to a tent to tune guitars, then took the stage. There were stage lights running off a generator or batteries, but they didn't carry far; the crowd stretched in the darkness out toward the hills as far as the eye could see.

The shows on that tour started with 'Jumpin' Jack Flash,' followed by Chuck Berry's 'Carol.' They were into the third song, 'Sympathy for the Devil,' when the trouble started. A small explosion occurred in the crowd opposite stage right, followed by a disturbance, a lot of movement, flailing bodies in the darkness.

The Stones stopped playing, except for Keith, who kept on as if nothing had happened. Mick kept yelling his name and finally got his attention. He wanted to stop the trouble, so Keith stopped playing. Things quieted down and they started the song again, but before it was done another pocket of violence had exploded.

'Who's fighting?' Mick asked, but it was clear the Angels were doing the fighting, or beating, on civilians; nobody was fighting back.

'Either those cats cool it or we don't play,' Keith said, doing once again not just the right but the heroic thing. 'I mean, there's not that many of 'em.' Then, pointing to one who at that moment was slamming into someone at stage left, Keith said, 'That guy there. If he doesn't stop it—' And the violence did, for the moment, cease. At this point I climbed onto a truck that was parked rear-end-wards behind the stage. Higher vantage point, safer, better view. Mick had tried offering the Social Contract, but clearly this crowd was not ready for the Enlightenment.

The Stones got things going once again by playing the Elmore James/Jimmy Reed 'Sun Is Shining,' a slow blues from the Crawdaddy days; but before the next song, 'Stray Cats,' could start, another pocket of fighting erupted. When the following song, 'Love In Vain,' ended, Mick asked that everybody sit down, and many people did. He'd tried to treat them like adults, each responsible for himself, but there was, as Keith said, no hope of anarchy.

Having attempted to gain some degree of control, Mick started singing 'Under My Thumb.' In front of stage left, a tall young black man in a green suit, standing with a blonde girl – I'd noticed him before, an Angel at the stage apron shoving him back – was waving a nickle-plated revolver. Then he was stabbed by an Angel who jumped up in the air holding a knife and came down on the black boy, carrying him by the force of the attack out of sight from the stage behind a mountain of speakers.

Things did quiet down after that, though none of us around the stage knew what had become of the black boy. The Stones played 'Brown Sugar' next at Mick Taylor's request, went on to play one of the greatest concerts of their career. And got out alive, the Stones, Gram, all of us jammed aboard one overcrowded helicopter. Keith said the Angels were 'homicidal maniacs.' The next morning, back to England on Pearl Harbor Day. The last thing Keith did before we left for the airport was to write a note to Stu telling him that the Reverend Robert Wilkins, composer of 'Prodigal Son,' needed a new guitar. Keith recommended a Dan Armstrong electric.

Say good night to the 1960s. Mick has been known to deprecate Altamont's effect on history, but it was conclusive. Isolated festivals occurred – Hendrix played the Atlanta Pop Festival in 1970 – but that wave of history had crashed on the rocks. With the best will in the world, the Stones had inadvertently recreated Vietnam in California. The change in the mood of the universe, felt by all, had to do with their good intentions, their sense of omnipotence that became, all at once, helplessness. So much good, they thought, was going to come out of what they were doing, but it wasn't that simple. Even Keith and Mick's idea to release a double album with Chuck Berry, B.B. King, and Ike and Tina Turner from the superb shows on the tour fell on deaf ears at the record company, where they didn't know who those other people were. Finally the Stones released a selection of their own live tracks from the tour, under the title *Get Your Ya-Ya's Out*, a (typically humorless bonehead Brit) misreading of 'yass,' as in, 'Catch the gravy drippin' from his yass-yass-yass.' The 'greatest rock 'n' roll band in the world' couldn't even release the records they wanted. Nothing was as easy, as attainable, as it had seemed. That sense of possibility we'd had was lost, and none of us would ever be really young again.

CHAPTER 10

'Louis [Armstrong] frequently had the most colorful and detailed recollection of things that never happened.'

Al Rose *I Remember Jazz*

What followed was a string of deaths – Fred McDowell, Booker White, Sleepy John Estes, Packy Axton, Al Jackson, Jim Morrison, Jimi Hendrix, Janis Joplin, Duane Allman, Al Wilson, Pigpen, Charlie Freeman, Jesse Ed Davis, Gram, Stu. All too soon.

Keith and I had begun to dabble in heroin – when there was a decent Asian war, superb opiates were available; you had to be unselfish to oppose U.S. involvement in Vietnam – even before the tour that ended with Altamont. Now we had an excuse. The Stones and I went back to London, they played a couple of stage shows, and then we all seemed to sink into a torpor. Anita was already addicted. At Cheyne Walk, at the thatch-roofed house behind the moat at Redlands, Keith and I talked, listened to music, did drugs. At the time, registered addicts could get cocaine and heroin legally in copious amounts, enough that an addict could sell most of his monthly supply to Keith and still have plenty left to knock himself unconscious in the downstairs loo.

'My thing with dope,' Keith said, 'is like on the

connoisseur level. When I found cocaine and heroin, it was pure shit handed out by the government. I used to buy it from junkies that they gave it to. They used to give them cocaine, thinking that if a guy was on heroin that he needed the equivalent amount of cocaine to balance himself out. So you went to the doctor and said, "I'm strung out on heroin, man." Fine, just sign here, you got to fulfill certain things, if you move, so we can set up a new area for you to collect your dope in. But pure . . . pure heroin. None of this strychnine, none of this street shit. No cops involved. And pure cocaine. And of course immediately the junkie says, "I don't need this shit, this is money." So he sold it off. So that's how I got into cocaine. People think that it's a matter of recreation, and it ain't. It's a matter of, as I said before, the drugs to me was something like, to get the job done.'

The Stones were signing a new record contract, leaving Decca for Atlantic, hassling over the footage for *Gimme Shelter*, dealing with tax problems, the kinds of things neither Keith nor I wanted to think about. The only enjoyable work Keith had at the time was overdubbing guitars and mixing tracks for *Ya-Ya's*. I became reclusive; Keith would send a driver to beat on my door, and I'd go over.

One afternoon down at Redlands, Keith and I were on an Oriental carpet in the side lawn, enjoying the cocaine and sunshine, while fifty yards away, outside the high board fence, two men with chain saws trimmed a tree. Leaning out of an upstairs window, Anita said, 'Keith, Marlon can't take his nap; make them stop.'

We walked over and stood under the tree for about five minutes while the chain saws went *arngg!* until the men deigned to notice us and turned off the saws.

'Hey, man,' Keith said to the one who was lowest in the branches, 'my kid's tryin' to sleep, and you're keepin' him awake 'cause those saws're so loud. And I know somethin' about loud, 'cause I'm in the loud business.'

'Right, mate,' the man said, turning the saw back. 'Be done in a few minutes.' *Arngg!*

Back at Redlands, Anita comes to the window again. 'Keith—' The World's Only Bluegum White Man, Camille Paglia's hero, the personification of rock 'n' roll, who speaks his mind to judges and Hell's Angels with no regard for consequences, had, in the real world, no effect whatever on his common-law wife and two guys with chain saws.

There was a picture of Brian, framed in silver, on the dresser upstairs in Anita's bedroom. Keith and Anita seemed to confront reality without flinching. Anita had remarkable insight into the Stones, describing to me at length the magic of the Jagger-Richards writing technique. 'They sit and play guitars, or Keith plays, and he sings – just sounds, but Mick hears the words behind the sounds.' Anita was funny and smart and pleasant to be around. When she tired of hangers-on and junkies turning blue in the loo, she'd absent herself upstairs until Keith cleared the house. Keith kept his sense of humor; framed on the kitchen wall he had a letter from his lawyers telling him not to use drugs.

You felt safe at Redlands, inside the moat, but at Keith's Cheyne Walk house you never knew what to expect. Keith and Anita sat around half-dressed, friends came and stayed all night, we'd go to clubs with Mick and dance, and Keith who couldn't drive would bounce off cars in Lena, the Mercedes he kept having painted different colors, blue to orange to pink. The police were never far away from Cheyne Walk. If I tried to leave Keith's on foot they would stop and search me. This kind of attention inspired Keith to do things like going into the tiny garden behind the house and settling off industrial-strength fireworks. When the cops came Keith said there must be some mistake, we'd been indoors all evening.

The aftermath of the last tour left me deeply depressed; I

125

returned to Memphis where I had a house, before the next tour, in Europe. The Stones were accomplishing things; they were in the process of separating from Allen Klein and they had their own record label, headed by Marshall Chess, Leonard's son, the person who had filled Mick's record orders back in the early 1960s. Compared to seeing a stabbing up close, this didn't seem very interesting. Invited on the European tour, I declined to attend. I had more material than I knew what to do with already. But there was more to come.

One aspect of my disillusion was the discovery of just how hip the Stones were. Charlie is one of the hippest men ever to reside on this planet, but the others – Keith and Mick would talk about heroin, calling it 'horse' – even my high-comedy companion Christopher made fun of them. I felt, and still feel, that Keith is a kind of hero, but Christopher knew B.B. and Furry and what a really hip person was like.

Hip or just flash, Keith and the Stones were on the road the next fall after the Altamont tour, with Gram, Anita, Marlon, Bobby Keyes on reeds, and Jim Price on brass. They'd officially fired Allen Klein and hired a new business manager, Prince Rupert Ludwig Ferdinand zu Loewenstein-Wertheim-Freudenberg. Examining the Stones' financial accounts, Prince Rupert discovered that their best bet was to head for the border and become expatriates before the next April, when the tax year began. (The brilliant businessman Mick Jagger, had simply thrown seven thousand of his own English pounds away on a misdirected bribe attempt after the Redlands bust, and everyone else had failed to check whether Oldham, Easton, Klein, or anyone else had paid the Stones' taxes.) Off to the south of France they went after paying all the taxes then due. In France they have excellent wines, onion soup, great cathedrals and museums, beautiful

women, and a town called Marseilles through which half the
heroin on earth passes.

'The one thing the English did for me was kick me out of
my own country,' Keith said, 'so I could really have to go
and live amongst other people, if I wanted to keep my band
together. I bless them ever since. If I go back and live there,
it'll be in Buckingham Palace.'

Nellcote, Keith's villa on the Riviera, became the location for
the Stones' sessions released as *Exile on Main Street*. They'd
had a truck equipped with everything necessary for a port-
able studio, and since there was room for everybody at
Keith's, and Anita was pregnant (after April 17, 1972, a date
on which Keith and Anita were together, there was Dandelion – who would become Angela in the less fanciful
eighties), and the Stones lived rather far apart, as a practical
matter it became simpler to stay and record in the basement.

Not everybody was happy with the arrangement; Mick
had dropped the heroin-addicted Marianne for Bianca Perez,
a Nicaraguan with excellent cheekbones. Bianca, whom
Andy Warhol called 'the greatest movie star who never made
a movie,' had been Michael Caine's girlfriend, and was used
to a crowd that was a bit more – well, a bit less rock 'n' roll.
Also, she didn't get along with Anita.

She, too, was pregnant; she and Mick married in May, and
their daughter Jade was born in October of 1971. Refusing
to stay at Nellcote, Bianca took up residence in Paris, forcing
Mick to commute. Keith, who saw nothing outrageous about
leaving rehearsals to put Marlon to bed and returning six
hours later, was furious when Mick would leave for a day
to visit his pregnant wife. Gram was on hand, even people
neither Keith nor I knew used our names – Newman (Ted)
Jones, a boy I'd bought a pair of trousers from at an avant-
garde clothing store in Memphis, turned out to be a guitar

maker, went to England where he met Jagger, went on to France where he met Jo Bergman and wound up as Keith's guitar supplier and maintainer; spent years working for Keith on and off the road. Made many times the money I've made from all this nonsense.

Having heard rumors about Gram singing on certain *Exile* tracks, I asked Keith whether that were true. 'No, no,' he said. 'I don't think he is on any – he was on some of the workups. No, Gram was just too much of a gent to impose himself that much.'

In spite of everything, the record was finished; *Exile* was released in May. Following two of the best albums in their genre ever recorded, the double album seemed scrappy, filled with bits that failed to cohere. That's what they said about *Naked Lunch*. Cutting in Keith's basement created a different product from albums cut in London amid topical hipness; the music reached back to Robert Johnson and provided an environment more varied (and more soulful, except for the Muscle Shoals tracks) than any the Stones had created before. Keith said later that he'd been in one of his heaviest periods of heroin consumption while doing *Exile*, which should tell anyone that drugs are indifferent substances that react entirely according to the individuals taking them – absurd to have caused Keith all the discomfort and expense he's suffered from inhumane drug laws.

Exile was – in content and packaging, with its photographs from Robert Frank's classic *The Americans*, whose introduction was written by Jack Kerouac – the Rolling Stones proclaiming their roots in the artists who preceded them. *Qua* gesture it may have been in its way at least as significant as the assemblage united on the cover of *Sgt. Pepper*. The Stones' previous album, *Sticky Fingers*, had been their first without any strictly English content; this one seemed American, out of the western hemisphere, down to the island rhythms on some tracks.

◻

The Stones' big, ugly 1972 tour started on June 3. You can see how a sensitive person like Keith might need medication, but none of this stuff cheered me up. I hoped for better things. The idealism of the 1969 tour had ended in disaster. The cynicism of the 1972 tour included Truman Capote, Terry Southern (would have included William S. Burroughs if *The Saturday Review* had come up with Bill's price), Princess Lee Radziwill, Robert Frank. Featured sideshows on the tour involved a traveling physician, hordes of dealers and groupies and big sex-and-dope scenes. I could describe for you in intimate detail the public desecrations and orgies I witnessed and participated in on this tour, but once you've seen sufficient fettucine on flocked velvet, hot urine pooling on deep carpets, and tidal waves of spewing sex organs, they seem to run together. So to speak. Seen one, you seen 'em all. The variations are trivial.

A boy who worked for Frank carried ounces of cocaine and brown Mexican heroin for Keith. I love heroin, especially that brown Mexican mud, and I said in my simple childlike manner – this was backstage at the Forum with Keith and the Stones and Gram and Dickinson – 'Man, did I see some brown Mexican heroin?' (The film-assistant boy'd just dumped some out for Keith, who was sitting on a couch beside that gorgeous black model girl with her black velvet bolero jacket and bravura britches with the Hank Williams rhinestone stitching up the legs – though close enough to touch, nevertheless at too far a remove to address directly.) 'I don't know, man, I swear to God I don't know what it is,' the boy said, about to go into cardiac arrest lest I should Mirandize him.

I visited the Stones in Nashville and on both coasts. The crowd around them was different – they'd been discovered by the hard-core beautiful people – but they were still up to the same thing. On this tour, the gospel singer Dorothy Norwood and the young Detroit singer Stevie Wonder opened for them. On the other hand, in Washington, at R. F.

Kennedy Memorial Stadium, I gave my seat to Sargent Shriver, who was running as George McGovern's vice presidential candidate. David Brinkley was at that show. I was wearing a pair of sea-turtle boots that showed up six weeks later on somebody else's feet as the cover of a rock album. This was the cocaine-and-tequila-sunrise tour. People have written much rot concerning Keith's heroin addiction at this time – he was still doing odd toots; granted, the toots were of a size to sedate a Kentucky Derby winner, but it wasn't as bad as it was going to get.

Terry Southern, always a keen observer, wrote, '. . . when you hear the sheer, drifting lyricism of things like "Ruby Tuesday," "Dandelion," "She's a Rainbow," or the intricately haunting beauty of "2,000 Light Years" and "Paint It Black," one is amazed that Keith's body of work hasn't received more considered critical attention.' Mick's vocal track had accidentally been left off 'You Got the Silver,' from *Let it Bleed*, which led to the rediscovery that Keith could sing, and on the 1972 tour he inaugurated the practice of doing a solo at each concert with another song to Anita: 'I Need Your Love to Keep me Happy.'

The 1969 tour had been, compared with 1972, run on a shoestring by accident. Now even the straightest people knew the Stones were some kind of major phenomenon, and paid attention, but what bothered me was Mick. He was dressed all in pink, he looked like some sort of mime/clown, and he played the whole show, even the rape/murder songs, as comedy. There had always been a mocking element to Mick's performances, but the archness, the parodic element, had taken over. The humor eluded me. Still, the Stones played some small places where they sounded wonderful, places not too different from English ballrooms. But the atmosphere was different; there was not much to do but drugs.

Before the show at the L.A. Forum, the Stones, Gram, and I hung out, together again, at Michael Butler's house. Gram had been in New Orleans, where his stepfather lived, had had a motorcycle accident, gained weight, lost his glamour. On another night there was a birthday party for Mick, where Little Richard and Ricky Nelson and the Turtles and Peter Lawford and Jim Keltner and Jim Gordon (who years later was convicted for the murder of his mother) were all in attendance. At one point we were in a bedroom – Keith, Anita, little Mick and his wife Rose, Peter Lawford, Jim Gordon, and, among others, me – sitting on an enormous bed, and Gordon was talking about how he did everything for God, he didn't care about money or fame, and Pete Lawford, that sweet weak man, said, 'Yeah, cool.' Keith and party kept disappearing into the bathroom. Tony Funches from the previous tour was there that night, looking less like an invincible black God (it was he who kept us together at Altamont, God bless him), telling Keith, 'Man, I been hearin' some very disturbin' shit about you.'

'Don't worry, Tony,' Keith said. 'I just got into bad European habits early.' And then went into a little explanatory shit-faced lecture about how the tradition in Europe is, like, you'll see these haggard be-diamonded dowagers at like Baden-Baden, geriatric addiction, making the whole idea of slavery to chemical stimulation elegant, and not just patriotic but humanitarian, not to mention epicurean and highly artistic . . . Keith transformed everything into his own romantic fantasy, still does. God bless him.

Little Richard, his head wrapped in a black do-rag, performed that night, at that birthday party, till all those present admitted that he was the king of rock 'n' roll. Mick Taylor was wearing sequins on his eyelids. It was the beginning of Glam Rock. I turned up at Sunset Sound for a Stones session around this time and no one else came except Mick. I had a car (an Avis rental with a heater that didn't work), he didn't. 'What you wanta do?' I asked.

'I don't know,' Mick said. 'We could get some pussy.' I

had the same feeling I'd had in London four years previous, that nothing was happening, the gears not meshing. I let Mick off someplace that evening, I don't remember where.

One night in L.A. in 1969, Stu and I were at a restaurant, and he was talking about Stones tours, saying that in the early days he and the Stones, with one Englishman and one American, would tour twenty or thirty cities. *'That's* a tour.' Stage crew on the 1969 tour numbered less than a dozen I imagine. Richard Elman, who observed the following tour for *Esquire*, wrote that '. . . by the summer of 1972 in Fort Worth, Texas, they were trying to pass themselves off as a bunch of middle-class businessmen, possibly even with ties to the *ancien régime*, and they had developed this impressive list of nearly forty (and sometimes sixty) British and American professional gaffers, stage hands, light men, luggage men, sound men, bodyguards, advance men, secretaries, a makeup man, a production director, and even a young M.D. to assist them in the deception.' The doctor didn't know it, but the Stones – Mick, at least – had incipient exhibitionistic elephantiasis. I remember seeing Bianca by the side of the stage wearing a pastel silk outfit with matching derby and cane. A Stones tour was, to Keith, more than a costume party; the communication he and Mick had had was suffering from alienation. Keith was into music, not glamour, not fashion, and he didn't trust these new people.

When that tour was over – no human sacrifice this time – people were, if not dying, dropping like flies: Jimmy Miller, Andy Johns, Bobby Keys, all went past the point where they could work. Bockris quotes Keith: 'There isn't one producer who can handle the whole thing. You run through them like you run through gas in your car. You burn them out. It's a ruthless circle. Jimmy went in a lion and came out a lamb. We wore him out completely. Jimmy was great, but the more successful he became the more he got like Brian. Jimmy ended up carving swastikas into the wooden console at the studio. It took him three months to carve a swastika. Meanwhile Mick and I had to finish up *Goat's Head Soup*.' The entropy was, however, not the only enemy.

◉

In the meantime, at the end of 1972, Nellcote was raided, effectively ending Keith's career as a Frenchman. He and Anita had started spending considerable time in Jamaica, partly because of the music, partly because of the dope, partly because the list of countries that would let them enter was growing short. There were, though, disturbing suggestions that Anita was too openly familiar with their Rasta companions. Two weeks after the Nellcote raid, Anita was arrested in Jamaica for possession of marijuana. According to published accounts, she was beaten and raped in jail and released only when Keith paid a twelve-thousand-dollar bribe. The glamorous lives of the rich and famous.

Six months later Keith and Anita were busted at Cheyne Walk and charged with illegal possession of drugs and firearms. They took the kids down to Redlands, which Keith, falling asleep with a cigarette, promptly set on fire.

In August, *Goat's Head Soup* was released, and in September the Stones toured Europe. The album's packaging seemed to embody symbols that indicated the realization on the part of the Stones that they had sacrificed a goat. Brion Gysin had told a story about Brian identifying with a goat he'd seen and was eating in Morocco, and Brian had had a pet goat. Because of the legal situation in France, *Soup* had been recorded in Jamaica. Sounded and looked as if things were catching up with Keith. 'Angie,' another of Keith's odes to Anita, the big single from this album, became the Stones' first number-one U.S. hit in five years, since 'Honky Tonk Woman.' 'Starfucker,' which Atlantic refused to issue with that title, and 'Comin' Down Again' are more typical Stones material, the latter a Keith classic. 'Slipped my tongue in

133

someone else's pie—' You can almost see the cracks appearing in Keith and Anita's liaison.

◙

While the Stones were on the road, Gram Parsons, in California, waiting at a motel for Merle Haggard to come and produce him, overdosed and died. Phil Kaufman, a Los Angeles character who'd road-managed the Stones, followed Gram's expressed desire by taking him to Joshua Tree (stealing the body from a baggage ramp at LAX), dousing him with gasoline, and cremating him.

'Gram checked into one motel too many,' Keith said. 'Unfortunately. Amazing, the guy made four or five records, still he was a force, he was a definite force in things. A guy that made one record on his own, two or three with the Burritos, a couple with the Byrds. Gram was a special guy. Very special. If Gram was in a room, everybody else became sweet. Except Mick. He'd leave.

'The older you get the more proud you are of getting there, because you know that half the suckers down the road, they ain't gonna make it. The fatality rate is pretty high. We've seen our own friends drop at our very sides.'

Along about here, things started getting weird. Anita and the Rastafarians had been bad enough that Keith needed soothing in some northern European arms, and apparently he found that with a German model named Uschi Obermeier.

Parallel to this, a strange flirtation commenced between Ron Wood of the Faces and Jagger-Richards. Seems Jagger started hanging out with Wood, thinking that Wood might serve as a replacement for Keith (!) on a U.S. tour if Keith couldn't get a visa. That was sufficiently annoying to Keith – that his oldest friend and closest ally had a vision of the Stones whose guitar players would be Mick Taylor and Ron Wood. Then Keith met Woody and loved him, as anybody would. Fair enough. But the next Stones single, 'It's Only

Rock 'n' Roll,' written by Jagger and Wood (though credited to J-R) was the first featuring neither Keith nor Charlie; not a good sign. Then, in December – 1974 by now – two months after the *Only R 'n' R* album was released, and just as they were about to start recording another one, Mick Taylor quit the band. The next day, Keith, angry enough with Taylor to kill him, sent the following telegram: 'Really enjoyed playing with you for the last five years. Thanks for all the turn-ons. Best wishes and love.' Coals of fire. Later on, Keith said, 'I asked Mick, "Why the fuck did you do that?" And typical, à la Mick Taylor: "I don't know. If I could answer that one, Keith—" '

It's Only Rock 'n' Roll had a quality of acceptance about it and contained such treasures as 'Short and Curlies' and 'Fingerprint File.' Just because you're paranoid doesn't mean they aren't out to get you: 'And there's some little jerk in the F.B.I. keepin' papers on me six feet high.'

'Since *Exile on Main Street*,' Roy Carr said in reviewing *Only R 'n' R*, 'the Stones have been moving towards a point where they can operate without having to contend with transient trends. Basically, it can be seen that they wish to pursue the basic function of rock 'n' roll – to provide music for dancing.' Would God that they had stuck to this notion.

The Stones spent the first months of 1975 looking for a guitar player, a delicate matter at best, considering whom they already had. I mean, you wouldn't want Andrés Segovia: special talents, um, abilities, like joint-rolling, required – should not know too many keys, etc. This may sound flippant but it's the literal truth. Keith for all his apparent toughness has always been a delicate flower, aware of all the things he's unable to do. So fortunate were the Stones to find a superb musician who is as threatening as a sleeping cocker spaniel, one always willing to defer to Keith.

Among the potential candidates was the ex-Yardbird Jeff Beck, Mick Ronson, Ry Cooder, Rory Gallagher, and pre-Stones playmate Geoff Bradford. 'The competition was tense,' according to Victor Bockris. 'An American guitarist named Nils Lofgren, who would release an unfortunate but well-meaning song that same year, called "Keith Don't Go," wanted to try out for the band. According to Ron Wood, Richards answered his request by saying, "Oh, yeah? How much you gonna pay me for an audition?" '

Keith found no one suitable until the last day, when the American Wayne Perkins auditioned. He was all but hired when Mick suggested they listen to Harvey Mandel, another American. 'Then Ronnie Wood walked in,' Keith said, 'and any other consideration just collapsed. If a potential suicide, in a bar for his last drink before he jumped off the bridge, bumped into Ronnie Wood, now he'd be living happily ever after. You want a psychiatrist, go see Ronnie. He's a one-man suicide line. I could make a fortune selling tickets: Suicide Court – they'd come out in half an hour laughing their heads off, with a new vision of life. In a way Ronnie was very instrumental in straightening me out, because he's totally instinctual. He would put his ass on a hot plate nude without realizing it and then say, "Isn't this fun? You should try this." Ronnie thinks a good laugh is worth a meal, or five hundred meals. I've caught him once or twice when he wasn't too much fun, but I know him *real* well. He's a terror, Ronnie. It's all to a good end, to him it's – anything to get something together.'

Ronnie joined the Stones in April; the next American tour started June 1. They didn't have any new material, not even a single. The excesses of 1972 were abandoned in favor of excesses even more wretched. The Stones traveled in a specially formatted Boeing 707 and appeared on an unfolding lotus-shaped stage. During the show Mick swung over the audience at the end of a rope, Tarzan fashion. At the big finish, a self-inflating twenty-foot phallus rose from somewhere under the stage, Hell, perhaps. That was bad enough, but Mick wanted to come onstage riding an elephant. Keith, bless him, refused to come onstage in Memphis until Furry Lewis had played. A big black limousine with a motorcycle escort came to Furry's ghetto flat, took him away, and Furry's neighbors gathered there and stayed until Furry was brought back safe and sound.

The Stones, particularly Keith and Charlie, were very gracious, welcomed Furry and chatted with him. After his set, a friend asked him if he wanted to see the Stones. 'No, I don't care nothin' 'bout it,' he said.

That night, Keith, Woody, and a driver set off across Arkansas in a rented Chevrolet. Everybody else on the tour was flying to Texas, but Keith wanted to catch a little cross-country atmosphere. Naturally, they got pulled over by the cops, and Keith and Woody managed to wind up in the Fordyce (pop. 5,175), Arkansas, jail. Bill Carter, the Stones' industrial-strength ex-Secret Service Little Rock attorney, came to the rescue posting minimal bail. As Scott Fitzgerald said, 'All you had to do was pay some money.' Charges were dropped on a technicality.

The tour ended in August, leaving Keith with the usual postpartum depression, compounded by Anita's having been deported from Jamaica for a second time. They met in Los Angeles and, trying to get it right, made Anita pregnant one more time. By January they were in Geneva, Anita still pregnant, still strung out on heroin and cocaine. The baby, Tara, was born on March 26.

On April 20 – a year and a half after the last miserable album – the Stones released what may be their worst studio album ever, *Black and Blue*. The U.S. promo campaign – including a billboard on Sunset Strip – featured a blonde, bruised and in bondage. ('S&M was popular in the U.S. in 1976,' an English writer asserted. Well, it was the bicentennial year, the whole country was excited.) This is the Guitar Smorgasbord album, with the auditioning guitarists Mandel, Perkins, and Wood. It sounds like a Rolling Stones album – even Mick's Dolly Parton takeoff, 'Fool to Cry' – but not a very good one.

Between April and June, the Stones toured Europe. Anita and the baby were in Geneva. On June 6, Tara suffocated in his crib.

CHAPTER 11

On June 6 the Stones were scheduled to play the last of three concerts at Les Abattoirs in Paris. Keith, heroic as ever, insisted that news of Tara's death be suppressed in the show-must-go-on tradition, which was probably the best thing he could have done for all concerned. His playing that night, available on the *Love You Live* album, was of surpassing emotional power. Mick's no-nonsense business acumen gave him the notion – hearing Keith's transcendent performance in Paris and being well aware that their recording contract was coming up for renegotiation – why not make a live double album, three sides from June 6, one from a small club gig like the ones they played in the old days. Eight months later, they prepared to complete the project. Neither Keith nor Anita had become less addicted in the interim.

Canada seemed a good place to do the club set, since Keith wouldn't need a visa to get in. The first problem, when the Stones arrived at Toronto's Harbour Castle Hilton, was that Keith didn't show up. Four days later, along with Anita and

Marlon, in Keith straggles. The following series of events was strange. No representative of the Stones met Keith's party at the airport to help with their passage through customs. A customs officer found a small lump of hash and an ash-blackened spoon in Anita's handbag, kept the items for analysis, and permitted the family to enter.

Within a day, Keith had reportedly obtained an ounce of heroin and five grams of cocaine. On February 28, Keith was, it's fair to say, in a drugged stupor – and uninsulated once again, no guard outside his door, most unusual – when fifteen members of the Royal Canadian Mounted Police came in and, after considerable effort, having managed to wake him up, placed him under arrest. Faced with a charge of trafficking, one nobody had beaten lately, Keith found himself staring at a potential sentence of seven to life.

'Their greed screwed them up,' Keith said. 'They could have put me in jail for a goddamn many, many years. Suddenly these guys who thought this was a brilliant stroke are working the Yukon. It took them an hour to wake me up to arrest me. You can't arrest anybody who isn't conscious. They were dragging me around the room for an hour and I had just fallen asleep after five days up rehearsing and working, and I'd got my dope, and they found it.

'I said, "This is it, baby, bye-bye." I even asked them for a gram back. Fuck it. You got my stash, I'm a junkie, you busted me, I'm shivering already, I'm already goin' into withdrawal. Just give me a taste, give me a gram back. They say, "No way, so, now what you gonna do?" You know I'm gonna leave this joint and go score. I've gotta. So what are you gonna do, follow me and bust me again? 'Cause you know I gotta leave this building, this police station, and go get some dope because I'm falling apart. I've got a gig tomorrow. So is this what you want me to do? Is this what you want? Give me some of it. They said, "We can't do that."

'Actually, they wanted to give it to me but they couldn't. And they started to really feel bad. I mean, they're just guys, you know. I just laid it on the fucking line. I'm gonna go now and climb walls? I'm gonna go score. One way or another. You can try to follow me, but I might use some other tactics in order to get it.'

Even without the Mounties' help, Keith managed, however painfully, to survive long enough to receive aid. Such a media melee was created, with the Prime Minister's wife involved, that Mick got out of town, went to New York. When he came back a few days later, the Stones concentrated on rehearsing for the El Mocambo, where, as *Love You Live* demonstrates, they were hot.

'Our band is just as happy,' Keith told a writer for *Rolling Stone*, 'playing the El Mocambo as Madison Square Garden. If we could just play one of those every month to stay in shape. This system of tours and huge auditoriums is really a very unprofitable way of using the available energy. It can't go any bigger. It's going outdoors. It's only now that we can find a way to make it pay for itself, but also to be able to play sensibly-sized places where the music fits. Whereas, with any sport, okay, they build a special place for you to play that game in. If you play football, you go to a football stadium. It's strange. Everywhere else, they have their venues specially made for what they do. But there is nothing for us. So we have clubs like the El Mocambo, but that's not going to buy any of us a Rolls-Royce, is it? What do you do? Play for three years at the El Mocambo? It's not possible. There has to be a way to do it in between.'

On the subject of his current legal difficulties, Keith said, 'There's all this incredible rivalry that goes on between different branches of the legal department – even on the international scale. It's like, "If the English cops can't do the job, let's show them!" It's their show. I guess also by popping me, they think I'm worth popping a hundred and fifty, or two hundred ordinary people. It shows people that your police are really on the ball – "We're doing our job" sort of thing – from a public-relations point of view. For all I know,

143

the public-relations office decides who they go after, but it's always [press] coverage if you bust so-and-so.

'Police: They are basically in the business of crime, you know, and that's there in the game. There's criminals and there's police, but they're in the same business. They both think the same way. If there is a criminal mentality, there has got to be a police mentality and it has got to be pretty much the same, since they are in the same business. I mean, it's no different than a wholesaler and a retailer in dealing in the same product. It's crime. They are both in it and there is really not much difference except what they want to put on as a really good guise. But it's still the same job. It's big business.

'I can't believe that a government would spend two seconds of its time worrying about what rock 'n' roll band is coming to its country. But they do. They spend precious taxpayers' time worrying about it. They are really out to make rock 'n' roll illegal. Really, it would be illegal to play the goddamn music. That's the basic drive behind the whole thing. They are just scared of that rhythm. That disturbs them. Every sound's vibration has a certain effect on you. You can make certain noises that automatically make you throw up. And there is nothing you can do about it. Certainly, every sound has an effect on the body and the effects of a good backbeat make these people shiver in their boots. So you are fighting some primeval fear that you can't even rationalize because it has to do with chromosomes and exploding genes.'

On March 8, Keith's second day in a Toronto courtroom, it turned out that, inadvertently or not, the court procedure was violated by the presence of an American journalist. On posting twenty-five thousand dollars' bail, Keith was given back his passport. Fans cheered as he left the court, but he was dismayed, once back at the hotel, to find all his Stones mates making travel plans, putting as much distance between them and himself as they could. Keith was holding drugs again, and they were scared, but it still hurt Keith to be abandoned. But Anita and Marlon stayed, and so did Stu, since he never did drugs anyway and didn't have the slightest reason to fear the police, mounted or not.

That's how Keith and Stu happened to be at Toronto's Interchange Studios, where the Stones had been working on the tapes from the El Mocambo, on the evening of March 12. Keith would learn the next day in court whether or not he was going to prison, and he responded to the threat by recording five of his most soulful performances, country songs he'd been taught by Gram Parsons, tunes associated with George Jones and Merle Haggard, each sadder than the one before. These would be released on many bootleg tapes and, ultimately, compact discs, along with other Keith tracks, like his versions of 'Let's Go Steady' and 'We Had It All.'

Keith's case was continued, but it was clear to him and Anita that, so to speak, the jig was up. They could no longer be the world's most famous junkies. The choice was clean up or go to prison. Keith knew of a British doctor, Margaret Patterson, who'd cured Eric Clapton and Pete Townshend of drug addiction by means of an electronic device called a black box. Arrangements were made with U.S. Immigration for Dr. Patterson to provide Keith and Anita treatment at a drug clinic in Camden, New Jersey. The cure worked, but it didn't last. Nothing does.

'I always felt I had a safe margin,' Keith said. 'But that's a matter of knowing yourself – maybe just on a physical level, just knowing – I come from a very tough stock and things that would kill other people don't kill me. And to me the only criteria in any of this game called life is like knowing yourself, knowing your own capabilities, and the idea that anybody should think they should take on what I do as some sort of recreation or emulation is, like, horrific.

'But at the same time I'm forced to deal with that problem because I'm held up to be responsible. That's the name of the game. That's what they tell you. I didn't ask to be an example to other people. I don't know enough about . . . All I know is myself. And I am the only one I can actually trust. I have many, many friends and I trust them a lot of the way down the line, but when it comes to life and death, I am the only one I can trust.

'That's why I don't have bodyguards. The minute you pay somebody to take care of it you might as well kiss it off. It's bullshit. It's like buyin' a façade, you're not actually buying protection. You're buying what people think – "You ain't a star if you ain't got fifteen bodyguards around you." Bollocks. The only one that can take care of this is me. They can't save you, they'll jump. And if you've got a bodyguard you like and any shit goes down, you end up jumping in front of your bodyguard and everybody's tripping over each other and it's a total state of confusion. You know, "He's my mate." Shit's flying around and you just get in each other's way. Everybody should take care of themselves. I was number one on the death list for half of the seventies. They were making bets on when I'd go. A lot of people lost money on me. I did a lot of dope in defiance. You're gonna lean on me, I'm gonna take even more. That's me, you lean on me and my back goes up.'

Love You Live came out in September, and the Stones started working on tracks for *Some Girls*. The punk sound had come along, or come back, with bands like the Clash and the Sex Pistols, who professed to consider the Stones old fogies. 'Revolting,' Johnny Rotten called them – because they were so establishment. 'I wouldn't piss on Keith Richards if he was on fire,' said Sid Vicious, who will never get the chance. Mick said he'd been listening to punk records: 'I'm open to all musical influence. I'm influenced by everything. That includes everything I hear. Whatever I heard that year. The big thing last year was new wave or whatever, so I was into that. Not only into that, I mean I couldn't possibly listen to it before three o'clock in the afternoon, but I heard it, and was influenced by it to a certain extent, and it comes out in the album, I think.'

In *The Triumph of Vulgarity*, Robert Pattison, perhaps the most perceptive writer about the cultural history and significance of rock 'n' roll, observes, 'The Stones are experts at doing what all rock tries to do. They take what is commonplace and therefore vulgar and give it life and energy. It's hackneyed to have a *shattering* experience, and the world the Stones described in "Shattered" is nothing if not ordinary – ordinary life in New York, described in the tritest monosyllables. But there's nothing trite about the final product:

> 'Don't you know that the crime rate is going up,
>   up, up—
> To live in this town you must be tough, tough,
>   tough, tough, tough, tough—
>
> You've got rats on the West Side
> Bedbugs uptown – what a mess—
> This town's in tatters
> I've been shattered
> My brain's been shattered – splattered all over Manhattan.

'The Stones redeem their clichés with the manic energy of fun. The good rock lyric delights in the laughter provoked by the flat statement of unedited feeling. Children, comedians, and Shakespearean fools also have the gift of extracting laughter from observations so blunt that no one else has the ingenuity to make them.'

Describing Keith's earlier, drug-descending incarnation, Pattison writes: 'In Annie Leibovitz's 1972 photo, Keith

Richards . . . instinctively reproduces the death-pose of [English painter Henry] Wallis's [Thomas] Chatterton – eyes shut in languorous self-annihilation, one arm limply falling to the ground while the other lies across a chest exposed by an open shirt-front revealing the pale, erotic flesh of beleaguered youth. It is the pose of the low-class rock victim beautiful in his liberation from the toils of the middle class.'

Some Girls was a rejuvenation, a rebirth, Keith rising like a phoenix from the ashes of addiction. 'Miss You,' their first number-one U.S. single since 'Angie,' nearly five years before, and their first chart song of any kind in two years, exploited the disco craze, and 'Faraway Eyes' harked back to 'Dead Flowers' and the Stones' country roots. Keith was mightily chagrined, however, when Mick recorded a parodic broad-comedy country vocal on the latter track, cornier than anything you'd hear on 'Hee-Haw.' Keith has the last word, a heroic concluding statement, in '(I'm Gonna Walk) Before They Make Me Run':

'I'm gonna find my way to Heaven 'cause I did my time in Hell,' Keith sang. 'I wasn't looking too good but I was feeling real well.' The album sold eight million copies, their all-time best.

Some Girls was released on June 9, and the next day the Stones began an American tour. Halfway through 1978 already, but the Stones seemed to have regained their energy, enthusiasm, focus. Carrying no horns, just Stu and Ian Mc-Lagan to play piano, they played such small venues as the Fox in Atlanta, the Warner in Washington, D.C., the Palladium in New York City, and the Capitol in Passaic, New Jersey. In Memphis, Mick asked the crowd, 'Kin y'all do a Rebel Yell real good? I know y'all can. It's a real treat for us to come here, 'cause so much has come out of this town, as far as music's concerned.' As a tribute to Elvis Presley, who'd died the year before, they played a terrific version of 'Hound Dog.' Etta James opened for them, another heroin recovery story. Ronnie Wood had blown his septum, so he took his coke and a long curved glass tube into the bathroom. You didn't want to see what he had to do – (children, you who are thinking about using drugs) – grown men would puke, sort of thing.

'With Ron we managed to get back to the original idea of the Stones,' Keith said. During their troubled past they'd employed hired guns like Al Kooper, Billy Preston, Bobby Keys, and Jim Price, who had at times threatened to over-power the Stones' classic appeal. Keith: 'Two guitars has always been my particular love. This way, with Ronnie, it's back to two guitar players and one sound.'

Some Girls took the Stones back in another way, creating controversy that far overshadowed the 'Starfucker' incident. The Reverend Jesse Jackson called for a boycott of the album because of Mick's racist lyrics on the title song, e.g.: 'Black girls just want to get fucked all night; I don't have that much jam.' Elizabeth Taylor, Raquel Welch, and Lucille Ball, all pictured in what they considered a libelously unflattering manner on the cover, threatened to sue, after which Atlantic removed the offending photos. Nothing serious, but still the Stones were stirring up a ruckus, as in the days of *Beggar's Banquet*, or the Stratford Garage Incident.

In October, Keith appeared in a Toronto courtroom where he was placed on one year's probation for possession of heroin and ordered to continue drug treatment and to give a concert for the Canadian Institute for the Blind. Keith had befriended a blind fan, a young girl, making sure she had safe rides to their shows, the kind of practical charity that is typical of Keith. The girl, who in spite of her blindness could obviously get around, went to the judge's house and talked to him,

God bless her. In New York the night after his court date, Keith celebrated by sitting in at the Bottom Line with Nick Lowe and Dave Edmunds.

But Keith and the Stones weren't out of the woods yet. Still rocking, though. In December, Rolling Stones Records released a Keith single – covers of Chuck Berry's 'Run Run Rudolph' and Jimmy Cliff's 'The Harder They Fall.' The idea was to release it every year at Yuletide, like 'White Christmas.' Seemed a good idea if you'd had enough snow.

Nineteen seventy-nine began with January sessions in Nassau for *Emotional Rescue*, an album that wouldn't be released for a year and a half, during which there was much idle time for Keith – heap bad idea. The production would have advanced more quickly if Mick and Keith hadn't become, around this time, somewhat estranged, even as cocreators. 'Our arguments were fun arguments,' Keith said, 'songwriting arguments. I'd say, "I think this should be an instrumental," and meanwhile he's written an opera. This is normal songwriting – "I think they should be really sparse," and he's just put hours and hours and hours into writing these little mini-symphonies, every syllable, every beat, covered. But then it got hard to get into an argument with Mick without it spilling over into other areas. For me an argument doesn't impinge, intrude, on my personal feelings. It's one of the greatest things, 'cause usually something comes out of that argument. Not just head-bashing . . . at times Mick is a great arguer. But, um, it got to the point that every argument that started to come along was taken as a personal attack. And then it becomes difficult to talk about anything.

'Especially if you're gonna write songs. To me, writing songs is like making love, you need two to write a good song. Now and again, a guy can come up with a good bit

Keith on the 1981 US tour. He ripped a new tee-shirt every night.

1981, Madison Square Gardens. What Keith has is not grace, exactly, but whatever it is, it's very effective.

Keith and Bert Richards, New York City, September 1988. Estranged for two decades, Keith and his father now enjoy each other's company.

Keith, Tina Turner and Jack Daniels, backstage at the Ritz, New York, January 1983.

Keith grinning but not picking. February 1984, television interview with
Lisa Robertson.

Keith, inspired by the Winos at New York's Beacon Theater, February 1993, commences to trigger toe.

Keith and Patti gang up on Ron Wood – Stones party at Corso's, a Latin dance club on E86th St, New York, for the film *Let's Spend the Night Together*. February 1983.

'She's my little Rock 'n' Roll.'
'Patricia,' Keith says, 'is an amazing girl.'

Keith mangles a minor chord, Beacon Theater, 1993.

Keith in February 1993, having yet another ecstatic moment.

by himself. But I think a guy I have known longer than any other guy, and I still work with that guy, would be able to deal with that. If somebody says something to me I think needs redressing in one way, I'll redress it maybe a little hard. But by now he should know my style and he shouldn't take it so hard. It shouldn't be so personal. It's my way of expressing myself. It's not a personal attack.'

Fortuitously, Ronnie Wood had done a solo album, *Gimme Some Neck*, and he was touring that spring to support it with a band magnificently named the New Barbarians, magnificently manned by New Awlins drummer Zigabou Modeliste, jazz bassist Stanley Clarke, ex-Face keyboardist Ian McLagan, bad Bobby Keys, back from the dead, and, as it turned out, Keith Richards, ditto. The New Barbs, with the Stones as surprise guests, helped Keith pay his debt to the Canadian sightless, playing two shows on April 22 at Oshawa Hall outside Toronto that earned fifty thousand dollars for the Institute for the Blind.

Unfortunately for Keith, who'd had enormous legal and illegal expenses, the Barbs tour barely broke even. The drug troubles dragged on even after the concert for the blind, because the prosecution could still appeal Keith's sentence. In a statement read by his lawyer in June before a panel of Toronto judges, Keith stated, 'I have grimly determined to change my life and abstain from any drug use.' Grim is right. Around this time, Chuck Berry did four months in prison for tax evasion. After his release an interviewer described his incarceration – jailing one of the country's best-known artists – as 'surprising.' Chuck said it didn't surprise him at all.

Keith was not cheered when, in July, while he was in Paris working on the new album, a seventeen-year-old named Scott Cantrell, in Anita's bed at Keith's Long Island house, blew his brains out with a revolver. 'That . . . really ended it for us,' Anita said. Keith was indeed nearing the end of his rope with Anita, but he still did the heroic thing, hanging

151

on to his guitar: 'I'm so sick and tired,' he sang in 'All About You,' 'hangin' around with jerks like you.'

> You're the first to get laid
> And always the last . . . bitch . . . to get paid.

'If people were more responsible for themselves,' Keith said, 'instead of buying insurance and calling lawyers every time a problem develops – if you have a problem with an old lady and you have babies together, whether you're married or not, if you say, "Darling, I love you but I can't live with you any more" – why do nine people out of ten reach for the phone and call a lawyer instead of saying, "Let's talk this thing out." The lawyers will have you hating each other within a week because that's their job. Their job is, one side against the other. You don't have to take this thing to court, just call it love and talk about it. And deal with it. Say, "I'll take care of you, I'm moving out, I'll pay the rent here and food for the kids, let's deal with this between ourselves. Let's just be human about it." You don't need a fucking lawyer. He'll take all the money that I would be giving you.'

Speaking of things falling apart, in 1979 old-time Stones (Keith) associate Tony Sanchez published his version of *Elvis, What Happened*, titled *Up and Down with the Rolling Stones*. The book placed Keith at such events as Brian Jones' funeral, which he did not attend.

In October Canada let go of Keith's balls. The Toronto judges refused to reopen his case. For the first time in nine years, he was indictment-free, free at last. Except that he still had to fight with Mick.

'About *Emotional Rescue* time, it suddenly became him and me,' Keith said, 'and I don't understand how it got like that. I came up and said, "Look, give me the weight again, babe,

I'm ready. I'll help you out now." In all innocence. And it didn't occur to me for quite a while that Mick saw it as a threat. I think that's true, I *think*, from his reactions to it, after thinkin' about it for many years now, and goin' over it for a long time. I think Mick's both an intellectual and a pseudointellectual, but to me his timing's gone off. Like Brian and Chuck Berry, Mick's a nice bunch of guys, and you never know from one day to the next which one you're gonna meet. Mick is a weird mixture of people, and he's still tryin' to live with 'em all. There's a fine patina of siege mentality, and he's so concerned with age. Actually he thinks he can fight it by going backwards. To me the way to fight age is by going forward. Otherwise you're not gonna get any age on you at all.

'The biggest problem I have with Mick is, I say, "I'm the only one that will scream at you and get emotional, and that's what puts you off of me." I say, "Look, straighten up boy. You don't have to look back. You got to look forward." I feel I owe Mick. This is why I get mad with him. When I did clean up my act, okay, now I'm ready to shoulder some of the burden again. I mean, God bless you for taking it all on your shoulders and dealing with the day-to-day running the Rolling Stones' business when I was just out there playing the artist, the freaked-out artist. And getting busted like that. And he supported me every fucking bit. I mean, I ain't knocking the cat at all. He knows – my bouts with Mick are on many different levels, mainly probably because of the length of time we have known each other. It took me a few years to realize – after I came back in the late seventies, although the first seeds were planted almost straight away – but I didn't want to believe that Mick had got used to enjoying my part of the burden, that he could now control the whole thing from just himself, and it became the power trip. He got used to it and liked it. I've heard the shit from the john, which was like, "I wish he was a junkie again." Because I think Mick had got used to running the scene.'

153

Thinking of the days when Mick could change the lyrics to 'Wild Horses' in an atmosphere of total appreciation, Keith said, 'Everyone was trusted at that time. And now I don't think he can trust himself quite so much. It's insecurity with themselves that makes the desperation of people like that. "Until I am sure of myself, until I can make myself out, I can't let anybody else in, then I get really confused." In a way I understand, especially if you're goin' for that front-man gig, like with Mick. It's a hard gig, out front there. You gotta be able to – to make it work for yourself and do the gig, you gotta be able to actually believe you're semi-divine when you're out there. Then come offstage and know that you ain't. That's the problem, that eventually the reaction times get slower and you still think you're semi-divine in the limo and semi-divine at the hotel until you're semi-divine for the whole goddamn tour. That's where it gets mixed up. I can understand, especially when all you're doing out there is singing and leaping around, you tend to forget – that's rock 'n' roll, son.'

CHAPTER 12

'I asked [Spencer Williams] where he'd gone to school in New Orleans. He was obviously an educated man and had a polished manner not inconsistent with his having spent so much of his life abroad in London, Paris, and Stockholm. He told me he had attended the Arthur P. Williams School and St. Charles University. I told him I'd gone to St. Aloysius, and he seemed interested to learn that I, too, was a native of New Orleans. Neither of us knew, needless to say, that someday I would undertake to write his biography and in the process learn that New Orleans never had a St. Charles University and that the Arthur P. Williams School came into existence several years after he'd left town.'

Al Rose, *I Remember Jazz*

At his thirty-sixth birthday party, beset by Anita and assorted whores, he met, courtesy of Mick's tall Texan Jerry Hall, the Miss America Soul of Rock 'n' Roll, Patti Hansen. And I would wind up baby-sitting the babies; I kid you not.

But we'd have some rough seas on the way to that harbor – February 1980 headline, Ronnie Wood and girlfriend busted in St. Martin with two hundred grams of cocaine. Patti, a Lutheran girl from Long Island and a top fashion model, was the only stability in Keith's life at this point – Patti and music, his own Keith Richards soundtrack, and in March he moved boots and guitars into Patti's Greenwich Village flat. 'Patricia is an amazing girl,' Keith said. 'She is amazing to me because when I met her I could have gone either way. I could have gone back. Easy. I was reliving a second rock 'n' roll childhood.' June 1980, *Emotional Rescue* released. Mick leaves for long vacation with Jerry in Morocco, sending a telex nixing plans for a tour, infuriating Keith. 'Mick waits,' Keith said, 'until he's three thousand miles away from anybody and he just sends a telex saying, "I'm not going on the road." I got a letter. "Yeah, aw great." I mean, you could have told me this in person two days ago

157

before you flew away, I was there with ya, I know you didn't want to but you could have told me the final thing. Don't run away to do it.'

By the next October, when Mick and Keith started working in Paris on an album Keith thought would be called *Tattoo*, they were coexisting peacefully. For the moment.

> *'She's my little rock 'n' roll mama*
> *My tits and ass with soul, uh huh,'*

Keith sang in 'Little T & A' – a song that offended some people, who thought it sexist. It didn't offend Patti.

By the time what turned out to be *Tattoo You* was ready, the beast had to be fed, needed blood. Mick had to agree to tour, and he did it in the increasingly uptight, suspicious, substance-phobic manner he had arteriotically assumed. The album was released in August, the U.S. tour went into the fall, the next spring they toured Europe. The album was interesting in that it contained the best music ever played on a Stones record; unfortunately, that music was performed not by any of the Stones but by the saxophonist Sonny Rollins, who could eat any one of the Rolling Stones for breakfast – musically speaking – underwater with a split reed and somebody else's horn. There had been a rumor, actually, that Miles Davis had been called to overdub on the album – the same Miles Davis who once inquired, 'Who the fuck is Mick Jagger?' I told Michael Ferguson about the supposed Miles-Stones dates, and Michael, going suddenly Irish, said, 'Miles wouldn't even get out of the fucking limo.' Selah.

In 1982, after twenty years, Keith and his father saw each other and took up the relationship that had ended when Keith stormed out of the council house in Dartford. They met in London, and Keith took Ronnie Wood along for moral support. Bert was thirty-seven when Keith was born; when they re-met, he was nearly seventy-seven. They had little in common except dominoes and drinking, but it made Keith feel good to be back in touch with his father. 'There had been so many attempts for several years, a couple of letters back and forth in the late seventies,' Keith told Bill German. 'And I never expected it. I thought, when it happens, it happens.' That year the Stones were in Europe. Keith had written his father again and this time when Keith was near enough to visit, he received a reply.

'I was so scared to meet him, I took Ronnie with me.

'Now,' Keith told me, 'I bless the fact that he's still around to get to know. I mean . . . he can sit in the sun every day of the year. He loves the sun, my dad; he can't play tennis anymore, his legs have gone. He likes to be out in the open, to swim and garden and anything as long as it's outside. Because he spent his life in a goddamn warehouse. He used to get up at four-thirty in the morning and get back at seven at night. He had to go all the way to London and back, every day, until he retired. He had the same job before he went into the army and when he came out with half his leg shot up, he went back to it. One job all his life. Now I can understand what a disappointment I must have appeared to him, right around '58 and '59, when I was fourteen, fifteen, sixteen years of age. I turned out to be . . . like, "This is what I'm workin' my butt off for," this creep in rock 'n' roll luminous socks at the top of the stairs, bashing away at a guitar when he should be doing his homework. But my dad and me reconciled the moment we met, we just sort of went, ha ha ha . . .'

◳

Keith and the Stones began recording sessions for the next album, *Undercover*, in Paris, fall of 1982. Keith was ready to marry Patti, and with that purpose in mind went to New York; then, January of 1983, Patti's father died and the wedding was postponed. *Undercover* took a year to complete, nearly; it was released in November of 1983, and on December 18, his fortieth birthday, Keith married Patti in Cabo San Lucas, Baja California. Mick spent most of 1984 working on his own solo album, becoming so estranged from the heart of the Rolling Stones that he drunkenly offended Charlie, calling him 'my drummer.' Charlie punched him out: 'Don't ever call me "your drummer" again. You're my fucking singer.'

An interviewer, discussing the longevity of the Stones, asked Keith about the strength of the Rolling Stones, and Keith said, 'The strength of the Rolling Stones is Charlie Watts.' It's true. Much of what Charlie has played over the years is simple, too simple to reveal his excellence; it's in the fills, the offbeats, the turn-arounds, that Charlie shines. He and Art Blakey must be the kings of the tasty two-bar color change. Keith also said of Charlie, 'He's got a wicked jab and an uppercut and left hook. I would never want to get in front of him. He only throws 'em once every ten years, but when he does I wouldn't want to be in the way.'

In January of 1985, the Stones started cutting *Dirty Work*. Mick came in fresh from the sessions for his album, *She's the Boss*, which would be released in March, with no material to speak of for the Stones. Keith was offended, but his and Patti's first baby, Theodora Dupree, was born on March 18, so that cheered him up. In July, Keith and Ron Wood played with Bob Dylan at the Live Aid Concert where Mick sang with Tina Turner and, on video, with David Bowie. Ronnie finessed the Dylan connection.

'I got Keith to my house for the first night of Live Aid rehearsals,' Ronnie told Bill German of the Stones' fan magazine *Beggar's Banquet*. The problem was that neither Keith nor Dylan knew that they would do the Live Aid performance together. Ronnie told Keith Dylan was coming to rehearse the show, and Keith said that was fine. But when Dylan arrived, he asked whether Keith or Ron were going to attend the concert. 'Keith then began to strangle me,' Ronnie said. Fortunately the diplomatic Ronnie smoothed over the misunderstanding and they played the concert together.

'I did Live Aid with Bob,' Keith said, 'because Bob asked me at the last minute with Ronnie to do it. The rehearsals were great, but it was a hard gig. I loved the idea of it, but you're not gonna solve the problems of this world with a few rock concerts on a satellite deal and a knighthood to the guy that got it together. That's a little Band-Aid on a problem, like tryin' to put a Band-Aid on a rash.'

Things were bad inside the Stones ranks; Wyman played on half of *Dirty Work*, Charlie became so frustrated and displeased he left the New York sessions and went back to England. The real blow came in December when Ian Stewart suffered a massive heart attack while sitting in a doctor's office in West London – he'd been having respiratory problems for a few days – and died. When the album was released the next March, they dedicated it to Stu. Stu's death was a real, basic loss for the Stones, but Mick's decision to tour with a band of his own, doing Stones songs, made Keith furious. '*Dirty Work* was built to go on the road,' he told me. 'The amazing thing is that it bubbles under, at this sort of 110 level, every goddamn week; it's outdone *Undercover* already.'

I had seen Keith in 1986 at the First Annual Rock 'n' Roll Hall of Fame Banquet, where he inducted the original member, Chuck Berry. If anyone else had inducted any other o.m., the Hall of Fame's authenticity would have suffered.

'I'll tell you the weird thing about that night,' Keith said. 'The banquet's at the Waldorf-Astoria, it's like black tie. I walk out of the apartment with the old lady, I've got on the tux I wore once before at my wedding and a fucking bow tie, too; I thought, "I'm gonna get married twice to the same woman without gettin' divorced?" and suddenly I said, "Hold on, babe, give me the key, I got to go back in." I went back in and put on this Lurex green jacket with black leopard spots and then put the tux back on top. I didn't know why I did that; I just started to get stage jitters, I needed a prop. I thought I was gonna get there and like sit at a table and watch the format and get the moves down and figure out what I'm gonna say and then like an hour or so later I would get up there and present Chuck Berry with his award.

'When I got there I found out I was gonna be the first fucking presenter – inductor, I have to induct. They haven't told me anything about anything and then I've got this fucking statue in my hand that I've got to give to Chuck, he's in the wings. And I'm thrown up there with no job training and the music business sitting in front of me. Then I realized, no sweat, I've got this jacket on and this is rock 'n' roll – ' At which point, saying into the microphone, 'I dunno, I never inducted anybody before – ' Keith pulled off the tuxedo jacket, revealing the lurid Lurex leopard.

Keith came off the stage, walked over, put an arm around my shoulder, and said, 'I loved your book. But I don't say that to anybody else.' He did, though, in an interview with a music magazine, call it 'the only one I can read and say, "Yeah, that's how it was." '

The evening ended with a jam session, Keith, Jerry Lee Lewis, Chuck Berry, James Brown, and some other people, accompanied by Paul Schaefer and the World's Most Dangerous Band, Steve Jordan on drums.

By this point, almost everything around the Stones had changed. Only Charlie's marriage had lasted. Georgia

Bergman, the Stones' golden-era executive secretary ('overqualified,' Mick called her) had left after the 1972 tour – the one with all the pistols – and in 1974 a New Yorker named Jane Rose had started working for them. In 1981, when Mick decided to fire Rose, Keith made her his personal manager. 'Mick decided he hated her,' Keith said. 'He hired her, I didn't. I thought, "She's got seven years of my god-damn life in her filing cabinet. She's got mine, she's got yours, too," but they allowed Mick to have his way. If I had given up on Jane, I could have kept the Stones together, maybe. It got down to things like that.'

Georgia Bergman said, 'Keith made Jane his manager because the more power he gave to Jane the more he'd drive Mick crazy.'

Relations between Keith and Mick (whom Keith now called 'Brenda') were at an all-time low. Keith, hurt and angry – he'd said of Mick, 'If he tours with another band, I'll slit his throat' – completed projects with Aretha Franklin and Jerry Lee Lewis. (Meanwhile, Mick toured with a rented band. 'If he's not careful,' Georgia Bergman said, 'he could be the Rod Stewart of his age.')

'Jerry Lee, what a gent,' Keith told *Beggar's Banquet*. 'I'd met Jerry Lee once or twice before, but real briefly. I've been listenin' to him since "Crazy Arms." He's part of my staple diet. As necessary as vegetables are.'

At Los Angeles airport Keith chanced to encounter Chuck Berry, whom he hadn't seen since the Ritz in New York, where Chuck had given him a black eye. While apologising for the Ritz, Berry – accidentally – dropped a cigarette down Keith's shirt. 'Every time him and me get in contact, whether it's intentional or not, I wind up wounded,' Keith said.

Thinking of these heroes of his youth, Keith said, '. . . It's very nice and encouraging that they're still playin', and playin' so good . . . That's one of the things about music; it's a hand-me-down . . . Whether you sell a million records or never made one, if someone's heard you and you've turned them on to it, you've done your fuckin' job.'

CHAPTER 13

'[Jimmie Rodgers] remained in the Houston hospital for about a month, charming the nurses and keeping Mickey, his Boston Terrier, beside his bed despite the hospital regulation banning dogs. He returned to San Antonio in February, 1933, partially recuperated and with orders to remain at the Alamo City for at least a six-month rest. But, despite the doctors' orders and despite a prediction made two years earlier by Dr. I. W. Cooper that he could not live longer than two years, Rodgers decided to make a recording trip to New York in May 1933, knowing probably that it would be his last.

'His last recording session is one of the most heartrending episodes in show-business history. His condition had become so weakened that the Victor Company provided him with a special cot in the studio. At the conclusion of each recorded number, he would lie down until he regained adequate strength for another performance. He recorded almost to the very end; his last session was on May 24, two days before he succumbed in the Taft Hotel.'

Bill C. Malone, *Country Music, U.S.A.*

Chuck Berry had snubbed the Stones in England, thrown Keith (whom he said he didn't recognize) off the stage for excessive volume at a concert he was giving in Hollywood in 1972, and, as Keith has said, turned and hit Keith in 1981 when Keith tapped him on the shoulder backstage at the Ritz in New York – and dropped a burning match down Keith's shirt in 1983 at LAX. Keith remains a believer. 'Aretha Franklin, Jerry Lee Lewis, Chuck Berry,' Keith said. 'If you're offered the chance to work with people like that, to me there's no question; you say, "Yeah." "How much do I owe you?" you say later. All those little things – you dream it, it comes true, if you stick at it and if you hang in for the course.

'After the Aretha Franklin video for "Jumpin' Jack Flash" that Steve Jordan and I did together, Steve and I were flying back from Detroit to New York. The thing with Chuck Berry was starting to come together to become a movie, and Steve asked me, "Can I do the Chuck Berry thing if it comes together?" At the time I didn't know – me, dummy! – I said, "No, I don't think maybe you're the right cat for this." I really hadn't thought about all I knew about Steve at that point because I had seen him play with Carl Perkins, I had

167

seen him play in millions of situations. It was my own doubt. I was thinkin' about callin' Charlie Watts – I didn't know about this thing. I went straightaway down to St. Louis to meet Chuck and talk about who we're gonna play with and what we're gonna do. You know, "Don't hit me again because this time you're not gonna get away with it." There's a limit to hero worship.

'When I get down to Chuck's house, I'm staying for two or three days and Taylor Hackford was there. My first question was – without even realizing how important Johnnie Johnson was to the whole thing – like, "Is Johnnie Johnson still playing around town?" I knew he was, because Stu had told me before he died. Chuck says, "Yeah, he's still around." So next comes the really important question: "Will you still play together?" I think he called Johnnie the next day and Johnnie came, and suddenly I've got Johnnie Johnson and Chuck Berry.

'Then Chuck plays a videotape that he had shot himself – and when he was onstage a friend of his carried on shooting – a home video of the whole Rock and Roll Hall of Fame jam session, with Steve Jordan playing drums, but you don't see him in it. Chuck's playing this shit back to me at his house. Now Chuck Berry in his house has one of those big boom boxes, you know, with the two screens. One constantly plays the Playboy channel, these chicks with their tits out throwing custard pies at each other's face and like falling over logs and shit, sort of cavorting like twenties porno movies. The other screen is playing whatever Chuck wants to look at, but that's always there, he can always go to the white tail. This cat's got stereo. And on one side there's this home video, and it's rocking. We were rocking that night, and he says, "Listen to that fucking drummer. You asking me about drummers, just listen to that cat, Jack." (He always called me Jack. Many names for him came to mind. I presumed to call him Charles towards the end.) I go, "Fuck that, this is the man I said no to yesterday."

168

' "Chuck, can I use your phone?" I called Steve and said, "Changed my mind. Still wanta do it?" Because the minute I heard him, I said, Jesus Christ, no problem. He said, "Yeah, man, of course." I said, "I've got Johnnie Johnson." I could turn him on with that. I said, "But what's really fuckin' me up is bass," because we're talking about doing Chuck Berry's stuff up right, four to the bar, swing. We're not talking any bullshit eighth notes, as people conceive of rock 'n' roll these days – *boom-boom-boom-boom*. I said, "I'll be back in New York tomorrow night." He says, "Fantastic. NRBQ's playing down at the Bitter End and I think I know the cat."

'If a cat's any good Steve knows him – Steve knows the players, which is the area that I don't know, being stuck in one band for twenty-one years. You lose touch. Steve's like a directory of like the right cat for the right gig. Steve did jingles, he could write a book on the jingle industry, he knows every trick in the book, things I don't even know nothing about. He's an amazing cat. I mean, it was Chuck in a way that led me back to Steve again. It was a very ironic triangle in a way, especially when you consider that Steve thought that "Roll Over, Beethoven" was a Beatles song for the first ten years of his life. That's what turned him on to drums, and now there's Chuck Berry saying, "What about this cat?"

'Chuck came down to Jamaica, down to my place. He almost went into contortions, like heart attacks, very nervous. If you're not on Chuck's patch, baby, if Chuck ain't in control of every situation . . . and in Jamaica he was like a fish out of water. It started off from the airport when I went to pick him up; he can't even stand not driving, that's why he drives himself everywhere. He can't stand not being in control. Then he sees Steve again, he's already with me, I keep a drum kit in my front room. Steve is dreadlocked, so Chuck doesn't know whether he's a local cat or the cat that he suggested, because I've got three hundred Rastas around my house and they all look like Steve. If it's his patch, Chuck

169

will maneuver and manipulate anything, 'cause he can pull the switch at any time. To produce that kind of shit, you've got to be that kind of way. And then you get tested so hard that you kind of seize up. We're talking about Mick Jagger as well now. Chuck, Jerry Lee, these are all front men. It was very like workin' with Mick – that siege mentality, like, "Nobody is gonna get the better of me even if I don't have any fun."

'That's the price you pay for saying, "Nobody is gonna smirk behind my back saying 'I ripped him off.' " Fuck, millions of people ripped me off and I don't give a shit. You think so? If you can't get over that one then you've got a problem, and so in a way I was well equipped to deal with Chuck. And at the same time he's just such a mixture; even afterwards, the cat still fascinates me. I find him more appealing now that I know him better, than I did from him just hitting me in the eye or saying, "Fuck you, fuck off." I've known Chuck for twenty years before I did that movie and the best thing he ever said to me was "Fuck off." So I mean, hittin' me in the eye was like, "Maybe he's really serious." Let's check it out one more time.

'What scared me was not doing it. It would have been done anyway, and somebody would have screwed it up. In a way, it's still a bit of that missionary zeal. Here I am given the opportunity, on a plate – from my own selfish dreams, childhood, teenage rock 'n' roll dreams of, "If I could just be the cat behind Chuck Berry, playing the other guitar, if I could be that." Then it's given to me. Also, for twenty years, after all the fantastic records the cat just shucked everybody out playing live. Cheap, never kept a band, just blew everybody out. To have had the opportunity, maybe the last opportunity, to get some good live Chuck Berry – I ain't gonna get another chance to do that.

'Amazing to me, that I could put Johnnie and Chuck back together, because to me that is the team that made those songs. Chuck got the lyrics and Johnnie would give him the appropriate traditional melody to put it behind. Chuck would walk in with these incredible lyrics and Johnnie would say, "Well, the way to go is put some stops in it: Working at the filling station – *poom* – too many tasks – *poom* . . ." Then over sixty of them are straight twelve-bar boogies anyway, so it doesn't matter. How I first figured it out was because they were all in the piano keys. Chuck never even bothered because he's got such big hands; they are not guitar keys. If you were a guitar player writing songs, you would shift it down a notch or up a notch and make it easy to play guitar. I know Chuck's music like the back of my hand. When I had to do that fucking gig, that movie: E-flat . . . C-sharp? B-flat? Jazz keys, piano keys. If you're a guitar player, you take that E-flat and push it down to D or up to E because then you've got some free string to work with, some open shit. E-flat? I think I know my Chuck Berry shit and suddenly I have to play all of this stuff in these keys . . .'

At one point in the film, during the concert sequence in St. Louis, Chuck tells Keith while they're playing a song that after the next chorus he's going to change the key to B-flat. 'I was chewin' bullets,' Keith said. 'But my punch to his face was "No, we ain't changin' keys." ' Another scene records Chuck's difference of opinion with the engineer – with Keith putting in his money's worth as musical director of the film they were making, saying to Chuck, 'We're all gonna die, and it's gonna be left, and it's gonna be fucked up.' To which Chuck says, 'I ain't dying.'

'Better come to terms with that one, baby,' Keith said, thinking about it later. 'Chuck is so vulnerable in some ways and so – When he comes on tough and clams up, it's like a reaction, like, "I'm havin' too much fun, I'm letting these guys in too much," and he slams the doors. There were too many reasons for me not to do that gig. I know I've got to swallow a lot of shit, probably on camera, to do this, but if I can do it, if I can show that bit of myself, then at least everybody knows who the fuck I am. It's not a big deal, but if anybody wants to know then they can see a little bit more. Also, if I can go through that fire it can kind of harden me up to the point where I can admit to do my own record.

'Doin' this shit, bein' about to swallow bullets when Chuck Berry is tryin' to teach you some intro you know intimately well and you sold more records of than he has – in public, on film, in a full feature movie ... I'm gonna do this to myself. I'm gonna look like an asshole. In order to show the boys in the band – and Chuck Berry – that I'm serious. The boys in the band are going, "He's gonna knife him any minute and Chuck Berry's dead in his own house." I said, "No way, man. I'm just gonna suck on this egg and take this from the man, I'm gonna take this shit." I'm committed to getting this gig together – it's a broader picture for me than just whether I suck up to Chuck Berry or make a fight out of this thing, which would ruin the whole gig.

'I know no matter what I do he's gonna turn around and give me that condescending master look of "Not quite. Nearly, but—" because that is his weapon. I'm trying to use my weapon. My weapon is not taking the bait. That's where I got the motherfucker. What the motherfucker don't know is, when I made the fucking film and the record, his amplifier had nothing to do with what they had onstage. I took a slave amp and put it three sub-basements down in the Fox Theatre, a Boogie amp, and recorded off of there. It's got nothing to do with what he thought he had going, because onstage he keeps goin' up to the amplifier, boosting it. I didn't take anything from his own amplifier. I took it from the slave amplifier downstairs, where I had the sound controlled. I'm making a movie. There's millions of bucks riding on this shit and a gig riding on this shit, and I want to get it. Chuck would have appreciated that. 'Cause I did it up for him. The best Chuck Berry live you're ever going to hear in your fucking life. That was my gig and I was willing – he could piss on me onstage in order to get that together. He could have done anything to me. I don't give a shit. Chuck can't kill me – but he did help me live. And this is a good reason.'

In perhaps the gentlest scene in *Hail! Hail! Rock 'n' Roll*, Chuck and Keith play the Nat King Cole ballad 'Through With Love,' after which Chuck tells Keith, 'You should have been a jazz player. You play some pretty chords.'

'Nat Cole,' Keith said. 'That's where Chuck and I met. Chuck paid me the ultimate compliment ever in that one phrase. He can hit me in the eye again anytime. Chuck told me that at one time back in the fifties he had three records in the Top Ten, and he was in New York playing the Paramount, and Nat Cole was across the way at the Blue Note. "I just couldn't cross the street," Chuck said. See, Chuck fascinates me – he's an absolute asshole, but I've had lots of fucking experience working with them. And to me it's kind of a lovable trait. It's not a big deal that a guy is an asshole. It doesn't mean that you don't bother with him. To me, it's more intriguing than a guy who's fairly well balanced and has all the answers . . .'

[For the umpteenth time Keith reveals his traditional, his true conservative, view of history, here expressed in an analogy to 'By their fruits ye shall know them.'] 'You can be an asshole where pure gold flows and in that case, it's worth it. Perzackly. I mean it's a very . . . people are so bizarre . . . Chuck's working with Johnnie Johnson now. They toured South America together.'

It's worth noting that Keith's response to Berry's saying he should have been a jazz player was, 'No money in it.'

'If I hadn't played on the Chuck Berry thing, I don't think I would have had the balls myself to do the solo record. It was only through doing that and realizing that, hell, if I can face that and handle that . . . The singing part never bothered me. It's not the most beautiful voice in the world anymore but the Queen liked it. When it was at its best, before it broke. It's not been my job, singing, but to me, if you're gonna write songs, you've got to know how to sing.

'The solo record to me was – I failed to keep my band together. I feel guilty. This means I have to own up to myself, I have to look at myself in a mirror when I'm not shaving and say, "I'm going to do this, this to me is like the final insult." To make a solo record.

'We made the record as an excuse to go on the road. Spent two years finding these cats, and we started playing and looking for gigs immediately and at first it was, "Forget it. The only way you're gonna get gigs is to first make a record." That was what convinced me to make the solo thing go down. A lot of good guys. Ivan's real name is Aaron Neville, Jr. He's Aaron's son. He has another brother, Jason, younger brother, incredible singer – you could make a TV series, "Those Darned Nevilles," six-thirty Eastern, five-thirty Central time. Steve knows the jingle industry, all the different rates of being paid.... Charlie Drayton's dad, Drayton Senior, had been a jazz producer most of his life. Waddy Wachtel's a great session player. These cats grew up as musicians.

'What I look for amongst people in making it is like, "Okay, you play great and you play great and you play great, but if we all sit down in the dressing room, can we still talk?" Is it a matter of being a hired hand, has somebody got a hard-on against this guy that I don't know about? Or, do I find out that they are actually all friends? This I can use. This feeling of unity. This band, they've been through the mill already and they're just so super-talented. These cats know things I know nothing about.

'Another thing that is important is that they all had their own separate things going. So this is an extra to them. But to me it means that these cats already know what they want to do, and it's not like "this or nothing," an all-or-nothing situation. Everybody's got their own things to do.

Ivan's got his own record, Waddy's producin' stuff, Steve and Charlie have their own band together. Everybody in my X-Pensive Winos band has other things to do, it's not like they're hanging on my coattails.'

Wyman said once someplace that anything besides the Stones – you don't talk to Keith about it, it's just an interference; and Keith agreed. 'Yeah, to me everything else is like bullshit. Also, I could say, "I couldn't keep my band together," that's what it meant to me. But when you start making the record, then you get into it and you realize how much room there is still to grow. And then I ask myself, "What am I so scared about, doing something on my own apart from the Stones?" Was I just being chicken, was I just trying to keep the Stones together because I was scared of being left out there on my own? What was really my reason for this desperate fight? Was it that I wanted to keep in the cocoon and not break out, and that the fact I got forced out maybe has been a great thing for me?...'

CHAPTER 14

On July 28, 1986, Keith and Patti became parents once more, another blonde baby girl, Alexandra Nicole.

'You think about a lot of things when you have a kid,' Keith said. 'It's your little thing, and you think, "God-damn, I helped make that." And it's all full of purity and innocence, and it's just smilin' at you, and wants to kiss you and hug you and all it wants to do is just feel you and touch you, and you never felt so loved in your life. It's that bit of love you gave your own parents, the bit you don't remember – your kid gives that back to you. And you realize, "I've just been given the first two or three years of my life back." And then you say, "Well, what can I do with this information?" – apart from not shittin' in your pants. I always try to avoid that. But that is the comeback, and it's a vital piece of knowl-edge; it's like a missin' piece in a jigsaw puzzle. If you can keep that, instead of showin' them off – "Hey, I made this" – they made *you*. It's a reverse thing, because they give you that little bit – that important bit of living when you absol-utely don't know shit about nothing. Everything's a positive. 'Cause once you start to remember things – from that moment you start to remember, then you've gotta start makin' judgments. But in that early period, that first year or two, you can be whoever you want to be, the freest bird on this planet, just as if you was born a mole or an eagle, a jackal, a lion, a g-nu – g-nash yer teeth – or anything.

'If you would be bold enough to have a child – what they do to you is grow you up, make you think, "What the hell am I gonna leave behind when I'm gone?" It's throwing them into a fucking cauldron of pollution and fear. But a lot of people don't take any notice of their kids; they just think of them as a possession, or something like, "I fucked up that night, I forgot to pull out," and "Okay, we can do plenty more, if that one fucks up we can have another one – " We can be incredibly callous about ourselves. There are so many of us, and the forces of nature are relentless.

'You watch ants work – any other form of life – if we weren't here, this ball would roll very neatly and smartly for a lot longer. Which makes you think that maybe you don't belong here. We've put everything into gettin' off. Even, though it's probably paradise. None of the other choices so far look to me as attractive as this joint, but we're ready to suck it dry and shit on it in order to get a few off. We're just bigger ants. We're all gonna self-destruct, so put Adam and Eve out there on another trip. We've managed to perform this act in a few thousand years, the blink of an eye in evolution. You can look at it two ways, we're the joker in the pack or we're the little grain of sand that makes a pearl out of an oyster. But no other form of life on the surface of the planet needs art. That already makes us weird, as if it points a finger: "This place doesn't need them." This is why we're the only form of life on this planet that needs religion, that will actually kill each other over some abstract idea. We are totally at odds with the rest of the plants – apparently they like a bit of music now and again, they've grown to like it – but we're the only ones willing to kill each other and destroy the whole joint. We're sucking everything out of the ground, pushin' all this shit up in the air – and it's not like we don't know it. We know it. We're so fucking smart. We know it, but we can't stop ourselves. It's better to us to beat the other guy than it is to make things comfortable.

'That's the dichotomy between this planet and ourselves. We own it, we think. So did the dinosaurs, at one time, and look what happened to them. This thing's gonna beat us, if we think we own it. I don't see any hope for us, quite honestly. And I'm sayin' to myself, "I love my kids, what the hell am I puttin' them on the face of this planet for? Cut my dick off." And at the same time, I look at those girls in the morning when they wake up – "Good mornin' Daddy, give me a big kiss – I need this now, but what am I really handin' them?'

When Keith finished *Talk Is Cheap* and went to Los Angeles to make a video for 'Take It So Hard,' the album's first single, I arranged to spend some time with him there. In spite of having been with him in Cadillac limousines, Bentleys, rented Chevrolet station wagons, airliners, helicopters, bathrooms, bedrooms, courtrooms, in vast crowds, and alone, I was unprepared for the sight of Keith in an environment that excluded the Rolling Stones.

'When was the last time we saw each other – was it Memphis?' Keith asked, once we'd settled down on a couch in the small greenroom with Jack Daniel's, Rebel Yell, and a new band that looked at us as if we were a pair of fossils, which we were. Keith and I had started down the road to drug addiction together; we had gone to jail during the same years; we had, as he said a couple of days later, 'seen our friends drop at our very sides.'

Now we were together again with not a single other soul who was along when we started. It gave me a peculiar feeling. But two things were clear at once: the X-Pensive Winos were a real band – they finished each other's sentences like Donald Duck's nephews Huey, Dewey, and Louie – and

181

Keith was more relaxed and flying lower than I'd ever seen him. It cost us, in the old days, about a hundred times more to get through an evening. The psychodrama among Keith and the Winos was about on a 'Dobie Gillis' level, which made relaxing easy. 'What do you get when ya cross a pit bull and a redneck?' Wino Ivan Neville asked the room, then answered: 'A all-white neighborhood.'

Ivan, son of the classic New Orleans singer Aaron Neville, on keyboards; L.A. session guitarist for Linda Ronstadt and Emmylou Harris, Waddy Wachtel; Charlie Drayton on bass; Steve Jordan on drums – the Winos, who got their name when Keith found three of them hiding in a studio with a bottle of Dom Perignon, played every time the video people changed camera angles, even though the video would accompany the already-recorded master take of the song, 'Take It So Hard.' The first day was all rehearsal, but still the band played every take, because Keith was trying to get something started on that soundstage. The video was the least of it. He wanted to start a vibration in that room that he could carry across America and, if need be, the world.

For two days the only refuge from the soundstage was the little upper room where the whole band hung out. They demonstrated their willingness to play as long as they had breath in their bodies. On the first day, Charlie Drayton, playing drums, wore a hole in his left hand, put on a Band-Aid and a glove, and kept bashing. The set was against the old familiar post-nuclear rubble backdrop, disaster surrounding 270 degrees of the soundstage's horizon. The band played on a little raised wooden platform painted black. Stagehands kept putting dust and ashes on the cymbals to create a visual, uh, thing.

During a break, Keith and I had a prosthetic discussion. When I first knew him, he'd had what I called 'rotting fangs.' Now he had fine white store-bought uppers.

'But hit me in the mouth,' he said, 'and it's like those *Nightmare on Elm Street* movies – "Freddy's back."'

182

Keith was wearing a sleeveless T-shirt that revealed what he called 'bruises' – deep fissures in his deltoids.

'From *what*?' I asked, and Keith went through the motions of shooting dope into his shoulder muscle. 'I thought, "They're just bruises, they'll go away in a week" – and I still got 'em.'

The first day ended well after midnight. Except for leaping around a few times, imitating Jagger's 'rooster on acid' dancing, making the band break up, I'd behaved myself. It was strange being in Los Angeles with Keith again – where we'd been so long ago – after so many years, so many scars and heartaches.

Next day, three-thirty, back to work. At the end of the first set, Keith and I started a conversation that continued while we walked up to the greenroom. This workday, the day of the actual taping, would go on till three in the morning.

Back at the soundstage, Mrs. Richards and the bitsy blonde bombshells Miss Theodora and Miss Alexandra showed up from Disneyland. Patti brings with her an aura of sunshine, beaches, ponies, health, good things. From the 1961 Wurlitzer electric piano in the makeup room, down the hall from the greenroom, I babysat the sleeping princesses, worn out by the Magic Kingdom, while Patti stayed on the soundstage to hear Keith play. 'I haven't heard him live since he was finishing *Dirty Work*,' she said, 'and there was a lot of anger then.'

At three, when the taping ended, the crew gave Keith and the band a standing ovation.

'Where are the *niggers*?' Keith asked a bit later, as we waited for the rest of the band so we could leave in the limo. 'I got three niggers, a Jew, and an Indian to record us; I got it covered.'

The next day Keith and I sat and talked in his suite at the Mondrian on Sunset Boulevard, a crazy modern-art hotel, its design derived from the geometric shapes and primary colors of Piet Mondrian: flashy, but small rooms.

The night before, I'd given Keith a copy of a piece I'd

written about Phineas Newborn, a jazz pianist we both admire, and the first thing I asked was whether he'd had a chance to look at it. On his own for the first time, with many people depending on him, about to push himself to the limit for months to come, Keith, asked if he's had time to read my work, of course answers yes.

'Just the first few lines, before the phones started ringin'. But I thought – I'd like to know what kind of day it was. You just got the guy goin' down in the grave, it seemed to me a little *stark*.'

A person like this, you have to hug. Once I went so far as to kiss Keith on an airplane. An advertising executive in a white shirt and a red necktie had told him, 'The world isn't perfect,' and Keith had said, 'No, the world *is* perfect.' Under the circumstances, and considering what I'd been doing in the bathroom, it seemed a heroic thing to say, and I kissed Keith on top of the head, a gesture of blessing that didn't even bring a pause in the conversation. We were on our way to San Francisco and Altamont.

At the Mondrian, Keith and I caught up on family and friends, living and dead, and even a bit of interviewing – my concept of which was, we both sit on the couch and tell stories and the one who lasts longest wins. We were rattling on when someone knocked. 'SHUT UP, JANE,' Keith enunciated, then said, 'Oh, that's probably my wife. We may have to cool it.'

Patti came in with the girls – they'd spent the day at the beach, and now they were home to spend some time with Daddy, but soon Keith was speaking *sotto voce* to Patti just offstage (inside the bedroom doorway), explaining how the band was over at A&M Studios and, 'Y'know, I can't just do the video and then not see them, they're expecting me to drop by.' Mr. Independence, Mr. Rock 'n' Roll Outlaw, was asking his wife if it'd be okay if me and Stan just go over there for a little while, y'know?

At A&M, a Hollywood sort of studio where they have

alcoholic drinks, Perrier, fresh fruit, and suntanned blondes, the Winos, produced by two Caucasians – Don Henley and Danny Kortchmar – were doing vocal tracks. Ivan did one, then Charlie, then Waddy, and then Henley went out to sing a chorus. They were doing background vocals, singing the word 'Shangri-La' again and again.

Henley noticed the dreadlocked Steve Jordan beside him at the mike, climbing into earphones, and did a *que pasa* take. 'Because you gonna put on your white, in-tune thing, and it needs my thing too,' Steve said.

'Your thing?'

'My black, street thing.'

At the first 'Shangri-La' Henley fell on the floor, laughing. 'Okay,' Steve said. 'You sing it. I'll just stay out here.'

'Take two,' Kortchmar said. Steve was doing steps around Henley, summoning up images of many more dancers and a big pot of hot water for the white fellow.

'I'm gonna sing and you're gonna dance?'

'Right.'

'Take three,' Kortchmar said. Henley sang, but when he finished, Kortchmar was dubious. 'Sounds a little stiff, Don.'

'That's 'cause I can hear footsteps and shit.'

Kortchmar called a break. 'If you want my idea,' Keith said, assuming one of my own favorite roles, the Tiresome Old Timer, 'which you probably don't, but . . . have you tried doin' it with everybody singin' at once? I mean, even—'

'Yeah,' Kortchmar said. 'It sounded good around the piano.'

For a few minutes, people in the control room talked about how good it had sounded around the piano.

'Even if you wind up takin' it apart again,' Keith said, 'it might be worth puttin' it together—'

Kortchmar looked at Henley. Henley looked at the ceiling. You could feel the blood-sugar level in the room dropping.

Jimmy Keltner, the virtuoso drummer, sauntered in with a guitarist friend and – since things didn't appear likely to improve, to catch the groove, at the studio – we four went back to Keith's. Keltner, born again years ago, never stopped drinking or doing anything else he'd done before; only now, as he'd explain, he was doing it all for the Lord. He'd spent the afternoon with Jerry Lee Lewis and said that the Killer was mighty sad about his cousin, Brother Jimmy Swaggart, getting caught with the prostitute: 'Jimmy's a fine man, he loves the Lord—'

Keltner went on to make a couple more pious statements, and Keith said, 'When you come to see me, man, leave that stuff at home.' Once in England, Keith had silenced a Keltner sermon with the words, 'I love God. But I hate preachers.'

'What'd I say?' Keltner asked.

'You brought it up three times already, and it's gettin' on my *tit* – I mean, a guy hangin' on a cross, what a logo.'

The Keith-Winos tour started off at the venue I'd suggested to Keith, the Fox in Atlanta, a small room with warm acoustics. When the band came onstage, the crowd gave them a standing ovation and never sat down until they got in their cars to drive home. Every audience on the tour did that. Keith and the Winos played to standing, dancing crowds every night. The bought people – in Shirley Watts' phrase – like Jane Rose and Paul Wasserman, were alarmed that the show in Memphis didn't sell out and had to be moved from a concert hall to a Beale Street club, but people don't understand about Memphis. When you can hear Al Green every Sunday in church for nothing, why would you pay money to hear Keith Richards? Memphis is a special case, which to the initiated didn't detract from the success of Keith's solo enterprise. In a way I'm sure Jane Rose was hoping that Keith would take off, be swept up by public acclaim as a solo star. If that happened she'd never have to see Mick Jagger again. Some New York magazine editors even told me that though they liked *Talk Is Cheap*, their rags were panning it because they wanted the Stones to stay together – as if the Stones weren't far beyond the power of any of them to alter, inescapably more than the sum of the individual members. The world's full of people who believe in black magic.

The tour's last show was at the Brendan Byrne Arena in Meadowlands, New Jersey. At eight-thirty, in a room back-stage, a TV set was showing 'Benson' with the sound off; a Christmas tree's lights were flashing. Keith was sitting on a couch, guitar and a couple of sheets of tablet paper, study-ing the lyrics of Little Walter's 'Crazy Mixed-Up World,' with its opening line, 'I'm a crazy, mixed-up kid.' A large black man wearing a Blueberry Hill bill cap, white shirt, burgundy pullover, light blue slacks, and brown tassel loafers snoozed in a chair at Keith's side.

'This is Johnnie Johnson,' Keith said.

The pianist on the classic Chuck Berry sessions opened his eyes and took my handshake between his warm, peaceful hands, which seemed the size of catcher's mitts.

I sat down beside Keith, who said, 'I gotta learn this song, I gotta sing it in about ten minutes.' He sang a bit under his breath, then said, 'No, it's not "jump and shout" in that one – doesn't matter really, I can change them around—'

Across the room on another couch a blonde was looking at a book called *Dinosaur Dictionary*. The actress Daryl Hannah, a blonde gazelle in jeans, skipped by Keith's couch to say hello. He had moved on to the lyrics of 'Run Run Rudolph.' When I noticed Bobby Keys in his Mac's Club Deuce T-shirt, I asked him if he'd known Bobby Vee when Bob Dylan was Vee's piano player.

'Elvin Gunn,' Bobby said. 'That's what Dylan called him-self then. Bobby Vee didn't have a keyboard player when I was with him.'

'What key's "Run Run Rudolph" in?' Ivan Neville asked.

'C,' Keith replied.

187

'You slept through all this stuff you was supposed to listen to,' Steve Jordan told Ivan.

'I wanted to play with this man,' Johnnie Johnson, rousing himself, said to me, nodding his bill cap in Keith's direction. 'I can play rock 'n' roll with this man. Keith! Chastity's gonna call before the show.'

'Okay,' Keith said.

'That's my little stepdaughter,' Johnson told me. 'She love Keith, when he was makin' that movie with Chuck Berry she was always up under him. She's thirteen now. Me and her mother going to marry. Yeah, I'm gettin' old to stay alone, I might catch some kind of chill.'

'In 1969,' I said, 'I was on tour with the Rolling Stones, and we were talkin' about this great pianist, Johnnie Johnson. I've listened to you for so long. I'm so glad you could be here.'

'Yeah,' Johnson said. 'I like gigs like this. It break the monotony.'

That night for the first time the four-and-a-half-year-old Theodora saw her father play with Johnnie Johnson and sing with black former girl-group singer Sarah Dash.

'Did you enjoy the show?' I asked her.

'I wanna be a black girl,' she said.

I asked her again, just to be sure, and she said it again.

CHAPTER 15

I hooked up with the chief, he invited me in;
he said, 'Heap big jam session 'bout to begin.'

Well, we rocked all night and part of the day –
had a rockin' good time with the chief's daughter May.

I was making some time, and gettin' to know,
when the captain said, 'Son, we gotta go.'

I said, 'Thass all right; you go right ahead;
I'll do the Ubangi Stomp, till I roll over dead.'

Charles Underwood

In January of 1989, the Rolling Stones were made members of the Rock and Roll Hall of Fame. Mick and Keith met in Barbados, kissed and made up, and started working on what would become *Steel Wheels*. It wasn't a bad album, and some of it was exceptional. The Stones toured the U.S. from the end of August till almost Christmas, playing enormous sports amphitheatres on a stage as long as a football field. Such a big stage, Keith told *Beggar's Banquet*, was 'necessary when you play places so big, so that you have something to look at, not just a circle of lights at the end of the stadium. You gotta upscale it, and get used to running around a couple miles onstage.

'This is basically a club band. Rock 'n' roll is basically a club music. Nobody ever dreamt that this music . . . I mean, not even Elvis. It sounds best in a club. It's very difficult to turn what is basically a garage type of music into open-air football stadiums, where it all depends on which way the wind is blowing and where the sound is going. You get a crosswind and some cat down the road gets it, and he don't even want it. He just got off the night shift and wants to go to bed. It's not an easy thing to play outdoors. But if that many people wanta see you, what are you gonna do? You just gotta go up there and do the best you can, using the experience and some of the best help available in terms of sound, and just plain enthusiasm. Because this isn't just the Stones. We're only five guys. There's two hundred cats out there working with us, and it's really a matter of teamwork.'

I saw them in Birmingham, watching in disbelief a Rolling Stones show where nobody danced. Sitting on steep concrete bleachers, if you danced you could fall a hundred steps and kill yourself. Mick stood in one spot like Larry Olivier and declaimed, one foot forward, hand on hip. I found it extremely depressing. The reviews were terrific, 'Stones Better Than Ever,' that sort of thing. Speaking as one who saw them in 1965 and 1969 and 1972 and so on, don't believe it. Even Sinatra has rust on his pipes these days. Nothing lasts forever. The frustrating thing about the Stones, though, is that they can be great anytime they choose, or anytime Mick lets them. It is Mick who seeks these unwieldy venues, enormous crowds and enormous amounts of money: two hundred million dollars for the *Steel Wheels* tour worldwide. In November of 1992 the Stones signed a contract with Virgin Records, three albums for forty-five million dollars. A new album is in the works.

'The Stones are kind of selfish bastards,' Keith said. 'They don't answer their fan mail except for Bill, and they've never done anything to suck up to the public or anybody. I mean, this is it. You want it or you don't want it. It's all gravy to us. As a band. It's like a band philosophy. It's all gravy. It's unbelievable. This is a band that expected to do four club gigs a week in London, for a year or two, to make a point about other people's music.

'Music was always my release. I grew up with the BBC, as the Beatles did. If you had a discerning parent, a parent that was interested in music – and my mum, goddamn, she ain't discerning about too many things, but about music she's goddamn discerning – and I realized that I only listened to the cream of the crop. I never had to listen to "That Doggy in the Window." Only by accident have I heard it. With the BBC, I listened to Beethoven and Mozart and Bach. I know they are great guys but when I was growing up that shit was too heavy for me – but I listened to it every day. And what goes in the ears, if you are at all musically inclined, you can't help it, it's going to come out.

'My mother would be looking for Django Reinhardt, the hour of jazz, she knew exactly where on the dial to go. She got that from Gus. His daughters were all actresses, could all sing or play something. So I would hear Ella, Sarah Vaughan, Nat King Cole, Billy Eckstine, Louis Armstrong, Louis Jordan – it was a house full of music. I very rarely saw all my mother's family together. There were always one or two there, one would be playing piano, one would be reciting or reading some passage out of a book – "You got to hear this" – and they read you the whole paragraph. What I love about them, to them it was just pure enjoyment, a great line out of a book or a song they loved. No pretensions about doing anything with it except for the enjoyment it gave them, sheer enjoyment of something without looking for any comeback, any remuneration. The enjoyment was payment enough. I come from that line of people.

'The interesting thing about music to me,' Keith told me, 'is that music has always seemed streaks ahead of any other art form or any other form of social expression. I've said this a million times, but after air, food, water, and fucking, I think music is maybe the next human necessity. Music is the best communicator of all. And I doubt that anybody would disagree, if they think about it, that a lot of the reason you've got some sort of – whether you wanta call it, "togetherness" – anyway, some major shifts in superpower situations in the last few years probably has an awful lot to do with the last twenty years of music, or just music in general. It's like the walls of Jericho again. In our time, communication just jumped the wall.

'The only thing I can do now, by gettin' down a very

rough road this far, is – without preaching, 'cause I hate that – to impart obliquely and with a certain ambiguity a little bit of what I know about life, and let it seep in. But there is a terrible tendency nowadays – I'm sounding like an old man now – but the opportunity we've opened up in the last few years is awful, predictably so: the opportunity to pose. It only reaffirms my knowledge that the music business, in any given era, is ninety-eight percent crap. If you know that, and can avoid the posing bit, it's not going to hurt you. You might not get anything much out of it, you might fail totally "making it," as they call it. But it's not going to hurt you to go for that two percent. But go for the other ninety-eight and you're lost. 'Bye-bye, brother.'

Asked about his motivation, Keith replied, 'America. It's all got to do with bringing cats over from Africa and forcin' them to live here and work in fields, in slavery. It's got to do with the crosscurrents of music, and of all the weird things that nobody thinks of when they need a bit of cheap labor. And they've never realized the ramifications, and the effects – all they want is now now now, money money money, cheap cheap cheap. Then you get a few hundred years down the line, and pressure forces you to free these cats. Meanwhile they've learnt all your shit. They've been growin' up, generation after generation, soakin' up your end of the music, harmonics and melody, and patchin' in their incredible rhythms, after a few generations of that plantation stuff went down.

'And in actual fact it's not just America, it's everywhere, because English colonialism was one of the main forces of all of this. You go to Fiji, it's full of goddamn Indians, Brahman cattle and sitars, and camera stores, guys with turbans on – you're lucky if you can find a native Fijian. These cats were brought there by the English to work, same as why Ghandhi worked for the first part of his life in South Africa. This is maybe the only good thing about the British Empire – that unwittingly, they crosscurrented the world and the genetics of it, the racial quality – they didn't mean to, to them it was just economics at the time, but what they actually did was they crossflowed us all.

' "No regrets" and "No guilt" are very broad statements. The guilt thing is – something you've done to somebody, and you think, "That was a mean thing, I shouldn't've done that." It might be a tiny, minor thing, it might be just snubbing somebody. And as soon as you've walked out the door, you say, "Why was I so cheap? Just because he screwed me over for a few bucks" – or for any reason – because he got the girl I was tryna hit on – trivial things. But I don't think you can get to this point in anybody's life saying, "I regret that I did this or that," because that means that you've really still got to check yourself out, and you can't look forward, you've still got to look back, and you don't know what it is you've fucked up, and you haven't redressed certain situations about yourself in relation to other people.

'Maybe this is something to do with the downside of technology and communication,' Keith said. 'When I started, the music business was like – When I signed with Decca their main thing was electronics, making the black boxes. Music was a tax break, and the pop music made the money for them to look good in authorities' eyes because they would use the money from the popular music to redo all of Beethoven's symphonies with the London Philharmonic with so-and-so conducting, or Segovia's Greatest Hits, and God bless it, that's just music the same as we're doin' and everybody's doin' – there's only one song. There's Adam and Eve, and there's only one goddamned song. It's just a matter of a variation on a theme.

'Now it really is a big money game, and the more money involved in something, immediately the more conservative people are involved – and the more people are involved, the fewer know what the fuck's goin' on. These middle-level execs that sold more baked beans than somebody in the Northeast area for four years running get thrown on the

195

executive market – and the next thing, what do you know, you've been transferred to some record company, and suddenly from baked beans you're selling records. To them it's all units, but the next thing these cats get into is going to the airport to pick up some star and the chicks – and suddenly they're blown away because baked beans was never like this. You'd never get the same thrill out of baked beans. But they still don't know what they're doin' so they look for formulas, any cheap formula. Which is, for me, being myself, the beauty of the record business. It's so fuckin' predictable. They're gonna go for the common denominator. So if I can slide in around behind their asshole – I know where their asshole is.'

Keith: 'Take it back three or four thousand years – take it back to that cat who found a bone and beat the bone on the rock . . . and started to yell at the full moon – and then you might have the original song – and that's rock 'n' roll.'

CHAPTER 16

At the dinner table one day she told us that the ONLY thing to do for a dog that was constipated was to give him an enema. I thought my mother's expression very odd for the next several minutes.

Flannery O'Connor

M*ain Offender*, Keith's second solo album, again recorded with the Winos, was released in 1992. Ten songs written with Steve, Waddy, Charley, or Sarah, it was stripped-down rock 'n' roll, with horns on only one track. Songs like 'Words of Wonder' seem to present Keith as the menacing rocker and the funny old fart – the one who throws cigarettes up and catches them in his mouth – all at once.

'If you want to learn an instrument, sleep with it near your head,' bluesman Mississippi John Hurt used to say. That is what Keith Richards was doing that night in 1965 when he dreamed, awoke to record, and fell back asleep to forget, what would become the best-known riff in rock 'n' roll and the immortal words 'I can't get no – satisfaction.'

Imagine waking to discover you'd written a song. Imagine that song becoming the anthem of your generation. Imagine living from your teenage years onward in a pressure cooker of adulation and condemnation. Imagine making millions of dollars while taking loads of drugs and having friends and colleagues drop dead by your side. Imagine spending a fortune on legal expenses. Imagine speaking your mind to angry, drug-crazed Hell's Angels and mean-tempered British magistrates. Imagine going to jail. Imagine getting out. Imagine being unable to keep your band – 'The Greatest Rock 'n' Roll Band in the World' – going, and having to start over in your mid-forties. Imagine coming out of this turmoil with two grown children, two young blonde daughters who take after your beautiful model wife, and a future filled with promise. A series of narrow escapes – the life of Keith Richards.

A small-boned man five feet ten inches tall, with eyes the color of Rebel Yell, a straight nose Romanized by his nodding out into a loudspeaker, lank black hair that has developed a dash of gray at the temples and a tendency to curl, and short wide hands and feet – Richards speaks in a mid-Atlantic drawl, like a P. G. Wodehouse character who has wandered into an Erskine Caldwell novel. He wears a skull ring because he saw mine in 1970 and knew it was cool, but he says he wears it to remind him of mortality, which may sound better. He smells about the same now as he ever did, like a guy who has much better things to do than bathe.

I met Keith Richards over twenty-five years ago, in a London courthouse. Since then I have been with him in many circumstances – among helicopters and Hell's Angels, at home and abroad – but never have I seen him waver in his determination to offer himself as a living sacrifice for a kind of human expression whose history he reveres and whose future he continues to represent. Richards' dedication to his brand of music is, at least in his own view, quite separate from his perceived role as an icon. The Rolling Stones, like sex, politics, and religion, represent ultimate mystery to the popular, or vulgar, or editorial mind. That he has never seemed to confuse himself with his image is to the credit of renegade choirboy Richards.

'Everybody out there has talent. It's a matter of whether

they're allowed to find out, or they have the time to find out what their talent is for. To me it's all instinct. I've realized lately – all the weird training I've had, the art schools and World War Two, a baby, Hitler on my ass – human beings are a fine machine and it's a matter of finding the balance between the brain and the instinct. Practical use of recognizing your instincts and recognizing your brain and bringing them into focus. Anybody can do that, they have a talent and then they can use it. If I've got a talent, everybody's got one. There's an awful lot of people that just use their instincts because their brain has never been stimulated. I would never want to go one way or the other – on the whole I would say most of the fuck-ups have come from the brain and not the instincts. The brain I think should be a softening influence on the instincts but the instincts should drive. Trying to reconcile the brain with urges that come out of millions of years ago, the way the brain interprets these instincts is . . . a heavy trip.

'Aerobics of the mind. If you start thinking too much you can talk yourself into anything, and usually, being the kind of creatures we are, we talk ourselves into the most destructive and negative and downgrade kind of things. "I decided I'm depressed." Maybe you should talk to somebody else. Not necessarily a cat who is gonna ring a bell after half an hour and say, "You owe me fifty dollars," but you know, maybe you should just talk to somebody else. See somebody who's gonna bring you up. All you gotta do is meet one cat around the corner and suddenly your life's changed.

'Music has a kind of open door on the question "What the fuck are we doing here?" because it can never really pose that question directly. It just like scratches your ears, irritates you. There's a certain mystery about it and it sort of activates a response, somewhere that nobody can quite put their finger on. The mysteries of the nerve centers' and receptors' portion of the brain, lodged in my skull. Music seems to be the art form that can convey the times almost immediately, if some

201

musician is there and able to do it. And it's a canvas that gets repainted every generation, every year sometimes. It seems to be more able to respond to what's going on within the mood of the population. It's the quickest response.

'Painters have done that now and again. Picasso and Goya, the Spanish. . . . But, I mean, by the time the canvas is actually out it's already old fucking news. Music now is becoming more important with the immediacy – It has to do with the delivery system. When music was just a matter of waiting for some cat that could play something to come into town, things would take some time, no doubt. But now that you can reproduce it, music has gone into a phase of art that painting hasn't reached. I've never been able to translate it into movies – it's a totally separate thing. You can say that the visual arts, TV and movies, are analogous to making a record. You can reproduce one performance and play it forever and you can make loads of copies and it can be playing worldwide.

Writing at one time was manuscripts, the printing press was analogous in its own time to videos now. They're all vehicles. In music, the song is the same virtually every time, that's the beauty of it, that's where Jimmy Reed was probably one of the most incredible of all because, if he had three songs in his repertoire after twenty-five years – I'd say he probably had two, and those would represent such a small change in sequence in light of the possibilities; because the vehicle was down to such a spare – this is the important thing. That the vehicle can convey some idea – a different idea over and over again without any basic change in its form. Ninety percent of Jimmy Reed songs are twelve bars, the other ones are sixteen, then maybe a thirty-two in there once or twice – "Honest I Do" is one out of the pack. Otherwise it's just straight-edge, stripped down, the same sound every time. It was a vehicle, purely a vehicle; he's just taking a different route each time.

'To me the power of that music, the power of the blues,

the power of people like Jimmy Reed and Muddy Waters is . . . this is what I mean when I say there's only one song. It's just how you sing it each time. "It ain't what you do, it's the way how cha do it." Clichés are the most beautiful thing in this world. They wouldn't be there if they weren't true. The cliché is there for a certain reason. When you say "a cliché," people take it as a put-down on a certain phrase, but it all depends on how you use it, otherwise it wouldn't be a cliché. It has an edge on it. If you can spin it and turn it around in a slightly different direction, it's like a diamond. Another facet reveals itself and could mean a totally different thing. Our vocabulary consists of clichés. We spout ninety-eight percent clichés all day. Cliché all day. "How you doing, man." "Come on, take it easy, babe." "Good evening, good morning, good afternoon, have a nice day, excuse me, I'm sorry, thank you very much," on and on and on. Most of it is automatic, but then a lot of us is automatic.

'I've had the opportunity, when things were going cool, to be a front man – I'd take the weight off, "He needs a drink, I'll cover your ass and do a little number," but basically my job has always been to keep the fucking thing going for the front man. Charlie and I pride ourselves that you could be half a mile down the Super Dome, Mick could be down there and he don't have to worry about the beat and the band. He can worry about monitors and other kinds of technical problems and shit, but he doesn't have to worry about that. He knows he doesn't have to keep looking over his shoulder. Like "Who fucked up and what went wrong there?" What-ever happens, even if the electricity goes out, Charlie will keep playing. And will keep the rhythm going so you can get people through a blackout or a brownout.

In my position, I observed all of this going down for twenty-odd years, and now I'm required to do it as well. In a way it's rather like I've been a long time at school on this shit because I've been watchin' this cat's ass for years. I've learnt a lot of tricks I would never have dreamed up. A lot of Mick is in me and vice versa. The thing is, to invite that kind of adulation and adrenaline, you've got to pull that much adrenaline out of the audience in for you to feed on it, and this is another chemical reaction. It's a crossfire of adrenaline, the whole goddamn gig. That's what it is. You get up there – I've got thrown up onstage just out of bed, *boom*. The minute you get out there, those people give you energy, and you're totally together. If you're on dope, they'll straighten you up right away.

'I'm a cat who sits down and plays "The Nearness of You," and a hundred people say, "If you ever make an album, that's got to be on it." I'm the last cat Hoagie called. Hoagie Carmichael called *me*. This the biggest compliment of all time. I'm in Barbados, of all places, '82. The phone rings. "This is Mr. Carmichael on the phone." Right out of the blue. See, certain people had listened to the tape that Bobby Keys and I did, him on sax and me on piano, of "Nearness of You": "It ain't the pale moon, baby, that excites me—"

'Hoagie liked my version enough to think of botherin' to call me. He'd got it through my lawyer who'd given it to Sammy Cahn who's loved it and given it to Hoagie. I'm playin' the wrong chords, my piano playing is abysmal, but he likes the way I flung it together. He calls from Palm Springs. This is six months before he died. He's eighty-six years old already, and he's calling me. In fact he called me to try to turn me on to like two hundred and fifty other songs he's written. "Barbados," he says, "I've been there, been to Barbados many times." He says, "Have you tried the local drink?" I said I didn't know. "They just keep giving me rum punches." He says, "Ask for corn and oil." Corn and oil is a certain kind of rum and – the oil is felernum. This is the liqueur made out of sugar cane. I can't believe this, he tells me about all these titles, "This one's with Famous Music," and then he gives me this little information about Barbados. This is like getting a phone call from Beethoven.

204

'I sometimes feel that what I do in my spare time has nothing to do with – Everybody who gets famous gets put into this position. Like what I do with my time off is a little more important than what anybody else does. They try to lay on you the philosophy that it's your responsibility because other people look up to you as a role model. This is the prevalent concept. Models – I married one. There is no such thing as a role model. The only model is the idea you got in your head about yourself. Looking for somebody else to set the example for you . . . forget it. If this race is going to survive, it can't look to other bits of their species that have been blown up by the publicity.

'You say, "Do I have a responsibility or do I not?" And where does the responsibility lie? Is it – because they bust me and hold me up as suddenly a bad example – there where the responsibility lies? Is it their fault? Because they could have left me alone. Or is it they were just doing a job? I know it ain't. I know any cat that busted me is looking for a promotion. And any cat that busted me suddenly went down the drain somewhere, going to the Yukon from working in Toronto, because they did it for the wrong reasons. He goes, "Yeah, I know this guy's taking stuff and if we bust him we got him nailed." Do you think I didn't know that? I'm a walking time bomb. I'm trying to raise a family. I'm trying to keep my band together at the same time. You gonna force this responsibility onto me – then that question of responsibility becomes something else. It's you forcing the question upon me. If you leave me alone, nobody has to know. And nobody is gonna emulate what I do in order to keep my gig together. And it's my problem, and I'll solve it in my own goddamn way. Let the quiet man work.

'It's not just that we're suckin' it out of this earth, we're also fuckin' up the bits we don't understand, that circle it – and the weird thing is that the holes they've made with all that pollution and shit is over the coldest regions and that's what's gonna warm us up; it's also gonna drown a few acres.

205

And even if you stopped it now, the effect of it probably – and they're not gonna stop it now, it'll probably be like twenty years – And when something starts to warm up, it's like permafrost, it seeps down, keeps warmin' and warmin' for years and years. So that's not my problem, it's God's. I love thee, Ocean. The only thing about the [His] Own Image thing is, who'd want to look like this?'

'When it comes down to the nugget, as I said to Mick, "This thing is bigger than both of us." You cannot deny the Rolling Stones. As I was really on a roll finishing *Talk Is Cheap* I got a call from the Stones saying, "Band meeting about getting it together next year," just at the time I've managed to forget this stuff, and I'm tryin' to finish this album. I've got everybody in town at one time, mixing and doing that shit and editing. Bless their hearts, the Winos, they turned me around. I said, "I ain't going." They said, "Yes, you are." I'm saying, "No way." And they're saying, "You are." Of course, for the Stones, anything, I can't say no. It's like, "Reschedule. I'm gonna go to London for a week."

'I would like to see a little more energy and balls out of the boys. I would like to see a little bit more of being happy just to be one of the Rolling Stones out of all of them – you can't live off the fat forever. I don't want to be pulled into not doing anything but still living off the fact that you're a Rolling Stone. You either is or you ain't, if you is you're gonna work with the Stones and if you ain't, then forget it.

'I can't go down the street without somebody saying, "When are the boys getting back together, man?" Guys on garbage trucks sing out, you know. Also to work for ourselves . . . I think they've gone through a hell of a time, like trying to get over Stu, really. It's one of the reasons . . . They're just coming out of shock, I know I am. And my way of dealing with it is to start working, it was the only way I could deal with it. It wasn't maybe the only reason for the Stones not going on the road behind *Dirty Work*, but everybody tried to take it on the chin because basically everybody could see Stu saying, "Don't start fucking boo-hooing when they put me down a chimney." I mean Stu lives – that's immortality. I can still imagine what Stu is gonna say to me. You think I'll get away with this? "Shut up, Angel Drawers." It's just as if he was there. In fact even stronger in a way; I mean, one could almost . . . get Christian about it. The guy sacrificed himself in order to save the rest of us, in my most biblical moments, I've thought about it. Actually, it was his band. And because it was his band, he got the job of driving around and setting up their amplifiers, and wiping their asses.'

'It's big wheels and little wheels turning around – you think you've done some good, and twenty years later you're told you did the worst possible thing for the human race. Everybody wants somebody to hang when things ain't goin' right, and since things never go right, ever, there's always somebody to hang. What's so hard about gettin' along – this is what I don't understand. To me this is a mystery. And they say, "Well, that's easy for you to say, Keith Richards, you been rich for years and years" – little do they know . . . how slender things have been. Multibillion corporations crash overnight – it's easy. Because everything's run on a shoestring – including society. To make it work, you're spending more than you're making, in order to keep it going, and you're always waiting for the debts to be paid.'

The Stones are recording at present, and will tour in 1994. On and on she goes, and where she stops, nobody knows. 'What do these songs actually mean? What are we talkin' about?' Keith said. 'I say, well, if you can get along with one person, then it's gotta be possible that everybody can get along with everybody. Somehow.'

INDEX

Note: The following abbreviations are used in the index: AP for Anita Pallenberg; KR for Keith Richards; RS for the Rolling Stones. Song titles are given 'in quotes'; record album titles are underlined.